PRACTICAL TRAINER SERIES

KOGAN PAGE

Management Development Outdoors

A Practical Guide to Getting the Best Results

BILL KROUWEL AND STEVE GOODWILL

KOGAN PAGE
Published in association with the
Institute of Training and Development

First published in 1994

Kogan Page Limited
120 Pentonville Road
London N1 9JN

© Bill Krouwel and Steve Goodwill, 1994

British Library Cataloguing in Publication Data

A CIP record of this book is available from the British Library.

ISBN 0 7494 1162 7   18625770

Typeset by Koinonia Ltd, Bury
Printed and bound in Great Britain by Biddles Limited, Guildford and King's Lynn

Contents

Series Editor's Foreword

Organizations get things done when people do their jobs effectively. To make this happen they need to be well trained. A number of people are likely to be involved in this training: identifying the needs of the organization and of the individual, selecting or designing appropriate training to meet those needs, delivering it and assessing how effective it was. It is not only professional or full-time trainers who are involved in this process; personnel managers, line managers, supervisors and job holders are all likely to have a part to play.

This series has been written for all those who get involved with training in some way or another, whether they are senior personnel managers trying to link the goals of the organization with training needs or job holders who have been given responsibility for training newcomers. Therefore, the series is essentially a practical one which focuses on specific aspects of the training function. This is not to say that the theoretical underpinnings of the practical aspects of training are unimportant. Anyone seriously interested in training is strongly encouraged to look beyond 'what to do' and 'how to do it' and to delve into the areas of why things are done in a particular way. The series has become so popular that it is intended to include additional volumes whenever a need is found for practical guidelines in some area of training.

The authors have been selected because they have considerable practical experience. All have shared, at some time, the same difficulties, frustrations and satisfactions of being involved in training and are now in a position to share with others some helpful and practical guidelines.

This book is a timely addition to our series. Bill Krouwel and Steve Goodwill draw upon their experience to give a balanced view of outdoor developmental training and provide criteria to help trainers to decide what best meets their needs. The whole area of outdoor training for management development is plagued with horror stories or accounts of high jinks, and this has led to considerable bias in opinion of its value. There are perhaps two key features which are often overlooked. Firstly, the word 'outdoor' does not necessarily mean out in the wilds – it could be on the sports field. Secondly, outdoor activities must be related to the learning experiences which can be gained from them.

The authors develop these key factors to cover a range of advice from how to develop simple exercises in the company carpark to how to check the credentials of, and negotiate appropriate learning content with, organizations which provide outdoor developmental training.

Not only is the book a sound guide, it also provides an insight to outdoor development which could well change some fixed attitudes and open up new and stimulating opportunities.

ROGER BUCKLEY

Introduction

While visiting a major training exhibition, the reality of the outdoor explosion was brought home to us. Every other stand, or so it appeared, featured photographs of sweating middle-aged executives abseiling down things, crawling through things and paddling across things.

Airbrushed full-colour brochures were thrust at us by fit looking people who heartily assured us that *their* organization had found the grail. Others, their eyes agleam with evangelical zeal, assured us that *they* were the ones with a fragment of the true cross. Adding to the feeling of fundamentalist enthusiasm were smart young men and women in camouflage uniforms, offering salvation by courtesy of the Territorial Army, surely the most unlikely contender in the MDO stakes. Uniforms, though, were not exclusive to the part-time soldiery, with many young rock jockeys wearing matching outdoor trousers, and brightly coloured sweatshirts with inspiring logos.

Then the truth dawned ... The organizations at the exhibition represented only a tiny fraction of the total MDO community. There are hundreds more, all clamouring for clients, all pressing their claims to being uniquely suitable to do *your* business.

There is without doubt a bewildering variety of choice in Management Development Outdoors (MDO) these days. There is also a high degree of hype. These two facts must cause many potential users of MDO to throw their hands up in despair and seek some other means of satisfying their company's development needs. This is a pity because MDO, when well matched to the needs of an organization, is an extremely powerful development tool.

9

Structure of the Book

The purpose of this book is to give actual and potential users some frameworks within which to make choices. In particular we will address the issues of:

- why, when, and when not to use the outdoors;
- the variety of outdoor experience and appropriate applications;
- theoretical bases and models useful in MDO;
- choosing the right provider for you;
- self-help options;
- managing the programme;
- evaluating the results;
- insights into course design.

We also intend to illustrate the above with examples, including exercises, with which you can experiment and some case studies from our experience, both successes and failures. In each chapter there is an 'Activity' for the reader to consider, which we hope will stimulate their thinking and deepen their understanding. There are suggested answers in Appendix 2, but other correct answers are possible – such is the medium!

Some readers will naturally read from beginning to end, but we have tried to write the book in such a way that a reader can dip into a particular section of particular or timely interest and still make sense of it.

We expect and intend the book to be of interest and value to the training specialist in the organization considering using MDO or for a consultant evaluating the medium for clients. It will, no doubt, also be read by other practitioners, if only out of curiosity, and we welcome their interest. They will hopefully find much to agree with as well as dispute and we would welcome their comments. We sincerely hope some readers will be new or aspiring MDO providers and we have attempted to include plenty to assist and challenge them.

Our Background

Thoughtful readers will ask how we are qualified to write about MDO. The answer is that in the early 1980s, and despite our different backgrounds (one a company training manager, the other commander of a frontline training unit in the forces), we were both gripped with enthusiasm for this exciting new dimension in management development. We felt that the outdoors at last enabled Elton Mayo's 'Knowledge through Acquaintance' to be achieved within a human-skills training programme.

Since then, our careers have led us via client-hood to becoming practitioners. On the way we made mistakes and learned from them. We now wish to help others avoid those mistakes. The least painful experiential learning is when it's someone else's experience you're learning from!

We are also keen to see MDO accepted as the valuable and useful training tool it is. Closely related to this wish is a desire to see a more informed and discerning approach from buyers. Too often programmes are bought without sufficient forethought and care, and when things go wrong the medium itself is often blamed.

There is not even a single universally accepted name for the medium, it being variously called OMD, Outward Bound, and other things. We prefer and have adopted the term MDO as being reasonably descriptive, having fewer apparent other meanings and because it puts Management before the Outdoors, which we see as fundamental in deriving the best from the medium.

A Qualified Success

We look back on the development of MDO with mixed feelings. We're still excited by what can be done with the outdoors and we're still working in it. But so much has happened since the early days. The market has grown immensely. The number of suppliers has grown with it. MDO is now very big business indeed.

With acceptance and growth have come some real problems:

- Product quality varies enormously (more so now than in 1980 in our view).
- Many people making a good living out of MDO have never actually experienced life in industry.
- There's little to guide buyers as to what's good and what isn't, and some simply want their people to have fun in the mountains.

Often people still don't use the outdoors to the greatest advantage. Some still see the medium as the message itself. 'Let 'em face a bit of fear down a cave, let 'em get excited hanging off a rope, let 'em be stunned by the scenery and get 'em stupidly drunk on the last night – they'll be a better team for it' is sometimes the attitude.

An extreme manifestation of this attitude, genuine and recent, was 'Tell us your greatest fear … right, thanks …that's what you'll be doing tomorrow!'

The growth of MDO has been so fast that the supply of thoughtful trainers just hasn't kept up with it, and there have been some hideously inappropriate courses. The original lesson – that it's a great medium for management development, but useless as a message in itself – is too often ignored. There has similarly been little time to encode good practice, and thus we see trainers and clients unnecessarily repeating the mistakes of the past.

In summary, what we propose to do in this book is to define a philosophy for the effective use of MDO. In doing so we hope to provide potential users, buyers, and practitioners with a more complete understanding of when and how to use MDO: what works, what doesn't, and why.

Acknowledgements

In writing this book a number of people have helped. Peter March of Derwent Outdoor Pursuits provided background information on outdoor qualifications, Tony Hendry furnished copies of the problem-solving cycle he developed with Phil Wright, and Chris Creswick was very helpful in providing clarification about the early years of outdoor development.

Nevertheless, any mistakes are ours. If there is one thing that makes outdoor programmes unique, it is the way people live with the consequences of their actions. That is what we are now preparing to do!

1 The Roots of Management Development Outdoors

▷   SUMMARY   ◁

In this chapter we examine the roots of MDO including:

- The outdoor strand:
  - military training;
  - outdoor education;
  - voluntary outdoor pursuits.
- The emergence of management training and development:
  - formal beginnings;
  - more participative styles.
- The merging of the two approaches to form MDO.

After absorbing this chapter, you will:

- Understand the roots of MDO, its component parts, and how it came into existence.
- Understand the difference between outdoor pursuits and MDO.

Nothing comes from nowhere. Most 'new' ideas are developments of something older. By looking at where something has come from we can reach a better understanding of it and how it can help us.

Looking at some of the blind-alleys and byways of MDO can also help us by showing us what to avoid. Experience is a good teacher. Learning from the experience of others is even better because it is free of pain to ourselves.

The Outdoor Strand

Europeans and Americans have always had a soft spot for the outdoors. Most of us can recall expeditions and wilderness trips with great happiness. Even some of the bad times seem good when viewed through the rose-tinted spectacles of nostalgia. This interest in the outdoors is especially true of the professional classes, many of whom spent happy childhood times at Summer Camp or Scout Camp.

While the Euro-American affection for things outdoors, ranging from backyard barbecues to Everest expeditions, may have a strong indirect bearing on the growth of MDO, there are a number of more directly traceable roots:

Military Selection Procedures

On a number of occasions, military authorities on both sides of the Atlantic have needed to expand quickly the size of their officer corps. During the Second World War, it was realized that all-interview officer selection methods were crude and inefficient with a wastage rate of around 50 per cent. As a result, a three-day selection course was introduced which included a number of physical tests to highlight the most likely candidates. This was adopted by the British Army, and later by the US Marines and other organizations. The tests were simply for assessment purposes, with no attempt to use them for personal or overt team development.

The beauty of these tests – known generically as 'WOSB' tests in Britain – was that unlike simple assault courses, they required creativity, intelligence and human-relations skills as well as the usual physical fitness and teamwork. (WOSB stands for 'War Office Selection Board', a body now long extinct. The term is pronounced as written – 'Wozbee'. For an excellent victim's eye view of the whole procedure, you are recommended to Fraser (1970).)

After the war, outdoor pursuits centres included ex-officers among their staff, and to provide a respite from 'real' outdoor activities, WOSBs were recalled and rebuilt. Others of the same genre were gradually evolved and so the short outdoor exercise, still a staple of MDO, was born.

The Outdoor Education Movement

In the USA, Britain, and to a lesser extent mainland Europe and Japan, outdoor education has emerged as a cohesive educational force, with specialist courses devoted to it at colleges, a network of outdoor pursuits centres ever-hungry for more staff, and funding from state and local

- Youth Movements: There is little doubt that in an earlier and less cynical age, organizations such as the Scout Association helped to build a positive public attitude towards the outdoors.

The founding of the youth organizations themselves was positively influenced by the progressive military theorists of their day. For example, Sir William Smith and Lord Baden-Powell, founders respectively of the Boys' Brigade and Scouting movements, both had military connections, although neither fitted the stereotype of the Victorian military man as rigid, rabid and reactionary. It is significant that Smith utilized voluntary discipline and Baden-Powell strongly believed in the need to build initiative within his men, rather than break their spirits.

- Survival Training – in its most real sense – had a great deal to do with the founding of the Outward Bound Trust, for long a pacesetter in outdoor education (see Figure 1.2).
- Kurt Hahn: A German educationist with firm ideas about the complementarity of physical, social and mental health, he was instrumental in founding schools which used outdoor pursuits   as part of the curriculum and also in setting up Outward Bound.
- Field Studies: During the 1950s and 60s a large number of centres dedicated to the teaching of geography were set up in mountainous areas. When they had spare capacity, many of them turned to outdoor pursuits as a useful sideline.

Figure 1.1 *The origins of outdoor education*

education authorities. In those countries where it is most advanced, practically everybody attends a residential outdoor pursuit course in their teens.

While its roots are diverse and sometimes surprising (see Figure 1.1), outdoor education has undoubtedly helped the development of MDO by:

- providing a physical and human infrastructure within which MDO could develop;
- fostering a positive attitude towards the outdoors as a training medium; and

Outward Bound is the name of a particular organization which offers reliable development and adventure programmes. As the world's original provider of such services, it is very jealous of its name. A sure way to annoy both the Outward Bound Trust and other providers is to refer to the latter's work as being 'outward bound' training.

The story behind the founding of Outward Bound is quite bizarre: in the Second World War, a major shipping company discovered that losses of young employees during the period between being torpedoed and being rescued were much greater than the losses of older men.

It transpired that this was due to psychological rather than physical causes – the young people simply did not have the inner strength that years before the mast imparts. As a result, the Outward Bound Sea School at Aberdovey was set up, largely – and successfully – to implant that strength.

Figure 1.2 *'Outward Bound'*

- evolving a theoretical basis around the psychological as well as merely physical benefits of the outdoor experience.

Voluntary Outdoor Pursuits

Ever since the well-to-do began to punctuate their Grand Tours of Europe with the voluntary ascent of various mountains, the outdoors has proved a magnet for those with sufficient leisure, money and mobility to enjoy it.

As Western living standards rose in the postwar period, so did the number of people choosing to spend their leisure time in climbing, underground exploration, orienteering, canoeing, and a variety of other strenuous pursuits.

Many active hobbyists – a lot of them managers or trainers – found that they would rather work at their hobby than their job, and sought ways to make this a reality. This resulted in a steady flow of such people into the outdoor education and MDO worlds.

Many of them brought more than just their outdoor skills with them. They also brought a fund of understanding of the wider world of work. This has made the acceptance of MDO much easier than would otherwise have been the case.

From observation, we believe that there is a noticeable difference between outdoor trainers with real experience of jobs in the workaday world and those who have come directly into the outdoors from full-time education. This is summarized below, although we would add that the table only applies in general terms: *a good instructor without outside-world experience is still much better than a bad one with it.*

Additionally experienced	Without additional experience
Unabashed by *executive hype* – the barrier of bull and bluster that some managers (usually inadequate ones) use to cover the fact that they're not very good.	Can be a little gullible, and believe that particular managers are important just because they say they are.
Can relate to the pressures that executives experience. Sympathetic to the fact that managers, too, have psychological needs.	Are sometimes strongly unsympathetic towards managers as a group, possibly even perceiving them as interlopers in the outdoor world.
Understand that exercises should reflect the actualities of managerial life.	Have an imperfect understanding of the harsher realities of managerial life.

The Management Training and Development Strand

We do not intend to write a history of management training and development. We do, however, intend to spend a short time examining this branch of education in order to understand how the outdoors came to be a useful medium in which to practise it. In doing so we make an arbitrary division:

- *Management training* is that branch of management education which deals with the practicalities of management – the 'science' side which might include the task skills to manufacture most efficiently, addressing the mix of capital, people, and materials in a dispassionate way. Through business games and the like, the outdoors has some application in this field.

- *Management development* is the branch which addresses the 'softer' skills of enterprise, developing managers' competence in handling interpersonal matters, getting the best from people through improved understanding of the human condition, and developing as an individual. This is the branch where the outdoors has been most used.

The theoretical basis for much management training and development goes back a long way, with Elton Mayo's pioneering work on the interpersonal aspects of management taking place in the 1920s (Mayo, 1933), and the 'Scientific Management' theories of F W Taylor (1911) and Henri Fayol (1916) predating even this by some years.

Surprisingly, the idea of giving more than just the most senior managers the opportunity to improve their skills away from the demands of the job is a relatively new one, not gaining reasonable credence until the 1960s, and even now only practised patchily in some organizations. Nevertheless, since the 1950s there has been a massive growth in management development, and today it is a major service industry on both sides of the Atlantic.

Over the years, management development has itself developed. In the *early years*, management trainers took their cue very much from the academic world and 'delivered courses' with much use of chalk-and-talk, lots of conceptualizing and theorizing, and no great focus on practicalities. Even today, there are some management colleges which possess training rooms comprising tiered lecture theatres, complete with roll-around chalkboards.

The 'delivery' approach depended very much on theatrical skills, and many genuinely talented performers trod the boards, charismatically peddling solutions to the world's training problems. Managers seeing such performances tended to be ecstatic about the dramatics, but often failed to improve their skills as a result. Not all the trainers reached the highest standard of performance, and many delegates returned to their organizations dissatisfied with their time away.

During the 1970s, more *participative styles* of training became popular, with much emphasis on case studies and business games. There is no doubt that this was a move in the right direction, and courses became times when both trainers and the trained were active in their participation.

As learning was often unpredictable – and sometimes had nothing to do with the espoused objectives – trainers needed to be more flexible. Some trainers enjoyed this and found that, through tasks, they could access and begin to deal with underlying business and human processes, not just the mechanics of doing business.

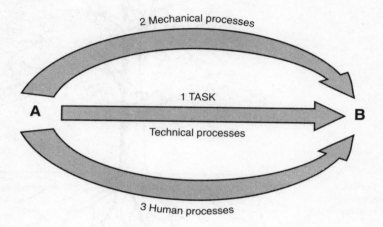

Figure 1.3 *The task/process model*

There was still some cause for trainee-dissatisfaction. Case studies, although based on real behaviour, lack the immediacy of real life. While very good for illustrating underlying principles, they are perhaps not so good at building skills for dealing with problems quickly.

Business games, on the other hand, have terrific immediacy, and are a wonderful way of teaching the fundamentals of business strategy, but often have very little bearing on the lives of those playing them.

Once it became clear that interpersonal *group process* was as important to business success as task skills, a variety of indoor experiential exercises came into being to ensure that management development programmes effectively addressed process needs.

These exercises represented a key step in the direction of MDO, because task reality was no longer present or even deemed to be appropriate. Thus, a group of managers might find that an exercise did not help them to learn the techniques of marketing, for example, but *did* help them to understand the dynamics of interpersonal communication, and even the hopes and fears of their colleagues. This can be illustrated by diagram as in Figure 1.3.

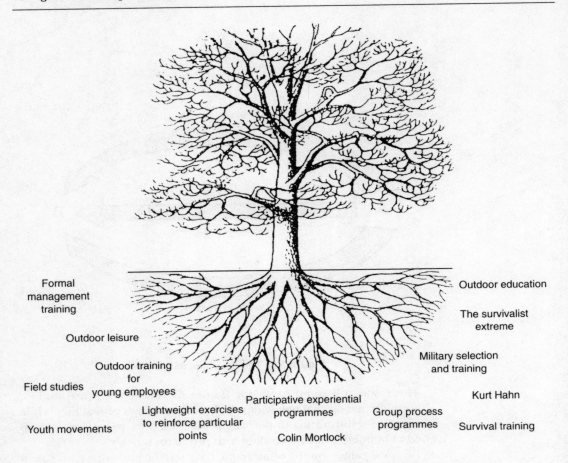

Figure 1.4 *The roots of MDO*

Figure 1.3 illustrates the conditions necessary for effective enterprise. In some examples from a factory reorganization, task skills are necessary to ensure that plant and machinery are put in the right places and are able to operate. Mechanical process skills – for example effective planning and communication – ensure that the executive processes underlying the move are taken care of, such as customers being informed of the times when normal service may be reduced. Human process skills are also important. Without adequate consultation, for example, people might feel threatened or hurt by the move, and fail to give it their full co-operation.

The Emergence of MDO

The *Task–Process Interface* is a key factor in understanding how the outdoors came to be used for management development. Once the need for (often spurious) task reality was dispensed with, all kinds of objections disappeared. There was no longer a need to be confined to the classroom; management training could take place anywhere. What became paramount were tasks with a high degree of mechanical and human *process* reality.

Trainers continued to live within non-existent constraints for a while, but like the apocryphal caged bear, gradually began to realize that the lock had been removed. One of the escape routes was the outdoors. A diagrammatic overview of the roots of MDO is shown in Figure 1.4.

Who exactly first made the connection between the outdoors and management development is difficult to establish, as it seems to have been synchronous to a variety of people in the early 1970s. Nonetheless, some key figures and organizations can be cited as prime candidates:

- *John Adair.* As part of the development of the concept of action-centred leadership (see Figure 1.5), Adair used a variety of exercises, some of them outdoors. His influence grew when his ideas were enthusiastically adopted and disseminated by the Industrial Society. His work was further developed in the early 1970s by many others, including programmes run at Brathay Hall for HP Bulmer & Co, a large producer of cider.
- *The Leadership Trust.* Such was the influence of the Bulmer programmes that many other companies wished to participate, and in the mid-seventies an organization, the Leadership Trust, was set up to meet the demand. This continues to the present day, using the outdoors almost totally in the service of leadership education.
- *Williams and Creswick.* In the early 1970s, Roy Williams, shortly to be joined by Chris Creswick, began experimental use of the outdoors as a medium for management development in areas other than leadership. At first they simply included outdoor tasks in otherwise indoor programmes, but later moved on to week-long residential programmes.

Their influence cannot be over-rated, not only because they pioneered the application of real management development disciplines to outdoor programmes, but also because they unselfishly energized many others – one of the authors included – to emulate them. Among other things, they established effective methods of review; they allowed groups to live with the consequences of their

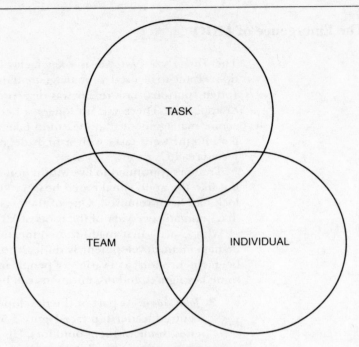

Figure 1.5 *Action-centred leadership*
(© The Industrial Society, after John Adair)

own actions; they designed exercises to address particular developmental needs; they used the physical but dispensed with the unnecessary and pointless cult of physicality.

It is fair to say that with Williams and Creswick, the synthesis of outdoor activity with management development techniques – MDO – truly arrived. Much of their methodology has become standard practice, often without acknowledgement, although the Williams–Creswick Window (see Figure 7.1 on p 90) is well known. Even now there are outdoor management developers who fail to reach their standards of effectiveness. In the 1970s they were a revelation – miles ahead of the rest of the field.

- *Early programmes for managers at outdoor centres*: A number of outdoor pursuits centres, principally Brathay Hall, offered outdoor programmes aimed at supervisors and managers. Initially, these were not very different from the standard programmes available for young people, but as time went on, they evolved into quite distinctive courses. Nevertheless, programme content betrayed their origins – starting the day with Cutter races up and down the lake, for example.

In a similar way, most Outward Bound centres offered adult programmes, and sometimes these were adapted to serve as management programmes. Some interesting clashes of culture arose, with managers refusing to be shamed into taking the traditional pre-breakfast swim!

We would add that Outward Bound, Brathay, and most other centres have moved on since those days. Nevertheless, be careful; throwbacks still exist!

Remember, nothing comes from nowhere. MDO is a compound of outdoor education and management development which works best when the components are almost equally represented. If one or other dominates, learning may suffer. Too much outdoors and delegates, literally, fall by the wayside; too much indoor work, and delegates talk of 'action-centred lethargy'.

ACTIVITY 1

One of the authors participated in a business game in the mid-1970s. He played the role of chief executive in which he opened and closed factories, cut prices, dominated the market, fought off tough competition, and generally had an excellent time. In working life he was junior training officer in a packaging company. In what ways might the game have helped his long-term development?

2 Why Use the Outdoors?

▷   SUMMARY   ◁

In this chapter we discuss the arguments for choosing MDO as an option for training.

- We explain the theory of experiential learning and how this applies to MDO.
- We examine the advantages of MDO over other forms of experiential learning.
- We suggest how MDO can be used most effectively.

After reading the chapter you should be able to:

- Understand the theory of experiential learning.
- Understand why it is more effective than other media.
- Understand the advantages and disadvantages of MDO, and how to ensure they are maximized.

The outdoors provides an extremely powerful medium for training managers in new skills or helping them to improve old ones. This is largely because outdoor learning is experiential in nature. It therefore makes sense to spend some time examining experiential theory and its application in the outdoors.

Experiential Learning

Experiential learning is a training method that seeks to move away from the chalk-and-talk, learn-by-rote methods of traditionalist education.

When considering the word 'learning', the earliest associations most of us make are with school, teachers and textbooks. School conditions us to think of learning as a process in which the teacher – the trained expert – has the primary responsibility. All the trainee has to do is absorb, memorize and repeat information as necessary. Much management training follows the same lines, with only cosmetic changes – flipcharts instead of chalkboards, handouts instead of textbooks – to mark the difference.

The idea that learning is merely about the theoretical is reinforced by the fact that textbooks – even this one – are essentially concerned with abstract ideas and concepts. Similarly, through long experience we come to expect that there is a special place where we go to learn – the classroom. This can also lead us to think that learning finishes when we leave full-time education, an assumption compounded by the emphasis on academic qualifications during recruitment.

As a result of the above we view training as a special activity divorced from the real world, concerned only with abstract concepts and possessing a predictable temporal end-point. Consequently, 'learning' is seen as a separate activity, largely irrelevant to our working lives.

Unfortunately this model is ineffective in a world where accelerating change is one of the few constants. We now live in that world, with career and job changes occurring at an ever-accelerating rate. The ability to learn quickly is now one of the most important skills that we can develop.

Experiential training has therefore evolved to challenge the old assumptions, and provide an effective means for people to continue to learn and develop throughout life. Herbert V. Prochnow wrote that 'Good decisions come from experience, experience comes from poor decisions.' We all learn from experience. By burning ourselves we learn to avoid hot objects, by testing our parents' patience we learn about acceptable standards of behaviour and the consequences of transgressing. Every day we have experiences from which we learn; education has even been defined as *changes in behaviour caused by experience*.

Some things simply cannot be learned from books or lectures. Examples range from riding a bicycle to falling in love. So experiential learning is a natural and constant life process which all development training, particularly MDO, utilizes.

Experiential learning can be seen as a four stage cycle (Figure 2.1):

1. concrete, personal experiences followed by:
2. observation of and reflection upon one's experiences, which leads to:
3. the formation of generalizations and abstract concepts, leading to:
4. hypotheses to be tested by future actions, which in turn lead to new experiences.

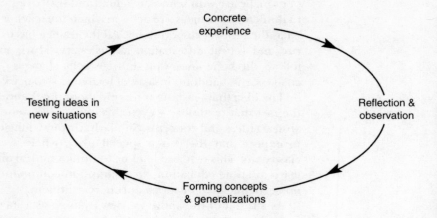

Figure 2.1 *The experiential cycle*

Those who do not learn from the mistakes of their past are condemned to repeat them.

A number of important things need to be remembered about the experiential model:

1. *The cycle is continuously recurring.* We constantly test the implications of what we have learned and modify our concepts as a consequence of what we see happening in each new situation. Most learning is indeed re-learning.

2. *The objectives we set ourselves govern the direction of our learning.* We look for and interpret experiences according to our needs and goals as we perceive them. Unclear goals lead to haphazard and ineffective learning.

3. *We all have personal preferences.* How we learn and which part of the cycle is most meaningful to us depends on who we are. It should be noted that overemphasis on one or more of the elements in the learning process can lead to ineffective and incomplete learning. Experience without reflection does not help learning; we would repeat experiences, rather like the rat which cannot find its way out of a maze because it keeps forgetting the results of its earlier attempts. Similarly, theory without the opportunity to experiment is limiting and sometimes justifies the oft-repeated blue collar jibes about college boys.

David A. Kolb has produced a Learning Style Inventory (Kolb (1976)) which examines these preferences in some detail.

A. The contract

1. The facilitator's intentions and objectives should be clear and open. All participants should understand that they are going to participate in an experiential exercise in which they will be expected to examine their own behaviour and that of others, and analyse those behaviours.
2. The contract should be simple, the number of experiences, the duration, appropriateness and objectives of each exercise explained and agreed.
3. The facilitator should be competent, prepared and trained to conduct the programme.

B. The activities

4. Participation should always be voluntary.
5. Aims for an exercise should be clear and shared.
6. The facilitator should present relevant theory when it is appropriate to the learning process.
7. The facilitator should be aware of and take into account his or her own needs and style and its impact on participants.
8. All experiences should be reviewed, with participants given time to identify the learning.
9. The facilitator should not initiate confrontation. It may be appropriate to encourage discussion or feedback on conflicts or problems, but confrontation should always be originated by participants.
10. Confidentiality of shared information is paramount, the facilitator should respect personal information and invite the same from all participants.
11. The facilitator should be prepared to seek and receive feedback on his/her performance.

Figure 2.2 *The ethics of experiential learning,* (Adapted from Johnson and Johnson (1975))

Galileo believed that 'You cannot teach anyone anything, you can only help them to discover it for themselves.' Similarly, experiential learning is based on three assumptions:

1. That people learn best when personally involved in the learning experience.

2. That knowledge, to be truly meaningful, has to be discovered by the individual.
3. That people are more committed to learning when they are free to identify and pursue their own goals.

Experiential learning therefore places the emphasis on:

1. Direct, personal experience.
2. Building individuals' commitment to development.
3. Giving learners as great a responsibility as possible for drawing conclusions.

An old campaigner in management training used to tell us 'You can't learn anyone anything' ... This is particularly true for experiential training, in that the responsibility for learning lies with the trainee, who therefore needs to be active and assertive in the learning role, while trainers should limit their role to providing effective design and a focus for reflection and the drawing of conclusions by the trainee. (To understand the trainer's role better, see Figure 2.2.) For example, if a delegate wished to learn about leadership they could take part in a programme designed to focus on that issue, reflecting on seen and experienced behaviour to decide for themselves what were the important lessons learnt and how they could best apply them in the future.

In a well-designed experiential learning programme, people will be encouraged to experiment, try new behaviours and to draw their own conclusions. Theories appropriate to the situation may then be presented to help them develop frameworks to fit their own unique requirements and environment.

The Motivation to Learn

How are people motivated to learn? Some see learning as worthwhile and enjoyable in its own right; others need extra motivation. Obviously it is different for everyone, but experiential learning stresses a sense of success and accomplishment in learning. Motivation is based on the desirability of the goals and the chosen methods of reaching them. Kurt Lewin (1935) identified four factors which lead to psychological success in learning:

1. Learners are able to define their own goals.
2. Goals are related to the learner's central needs and values.
3. Learners are able to define the paths to accomplishing their goals.
4. Goals represent a realistic level of aspiration for the learners – neither too high nor too low, but high enough to challenge and test their capabilities.

Feelings of success will only be fully realized when learners are encouraged to take as much responsibility as possible for their own behaviour. Many well-intentioned outdoor programmes fail because sessions are so tightly controlled that delegates feel more like passengers than active participants with jobs to do. Learners *must* at least have influence on, and preferably should control, the learning process.

Intrinsic motivation can be enhanced by other factors: The involvement of other learners in the process is often crucial to breaking barriers as is their approval, support and feedback – all can facilitate learning and increase the desire to learn.

Even formal theory has its place in experiential learning. Delegates often place greater confidence in their own learning when they discover that formal input supports it. There is no room for the set lesson in experiential training. There is, however, much to be said for inputting theory that supports the delegates' own findings.

The Advantages of MDO

MDO shares, but often increases, the benefits of experiential training. Indeed, many 'outdoor' exercises can be run indoors, given enough space and imagination. It is a sad fact that, to some, 'outdoors' means mountain ranges and untamed moorland. We have found that a car park or a hotel garden can be perfectly adequate places to run outdoor activities. Figure 2.3 summarizes the main advantages of MDO, some of which we cover here in more detail.

Reality

Indoor experiential learning is often based around role-playing or business simulations, with participants acting within some situation, as discussed in Activity 1. In that situation, one of the writers played the part of chief executive of a large company, making audacious strategic decisions, closing and opening factories around the world, and so on. At the time he was a junior training officer, so the exercise, while exciting, was fairly pointless.

This kind of thing *can* also be true of outdoor exercises, but it is much easier to set real problems with real consequences and real constraints. A team building a raft suffers a very real penalty if they do it badly. In effect, the task is real, although unusual. Its attainment encourages and usually produces interpersonal processes and behaviour which are typical of the way the team really operates. Participants are dealing with real people in

1. Transferable
The practical nature of the activities, where task accomplishment is easily monitored, where team results are measurable and where individual skills and contribution are developed can readily be transferred back to the working environment.

2. Complex
Outdoor exercises can be designed to any level of complexity, and allow scope for multi-layer management in any form and to suit any particular working culture. They lend themselves to related, yet separate, problems such as may exist between different sections of a business or industry.

3. Safe
- Physical safety; all activities should be supervised by trained and experienced staff.
- Business safety; course members can apply new techniques and experiment with new modes of behaviour at no risk to the company. Decisions and actions have no direct business consequence and accordingly activities can be tried which are not possible when at work.

4. Natural
Many traditional management training courses rely on delegates assuming roles to create a situation which has some reality to work. By using the 'here and now', out-of-doors exercises are designed without having to play a role, course members can be themselves and are unable to hide behind the excuse: 'I'm not really like that!'

5. Enjoyable
Most outdoor activity contains a significant element of enjoyment. People like to be involved, this leads to increased motivation and commitment to learning. They learn better when they are enjoying the activity.

6. Memorable
The drama and excitement of the outdoor activities will make a lasting impression. Recall of the activity leads to recall of the learning and its application.

7. Real
Perhaps the greatest asset of all. There is no artificiality in the exercises outdoors – the problems are real, the issues are dynamic, the constraints are felt, the people are live, the consequences are real. There is no need to act – it is the real world.

Figure 2.3 *Why use the outdoors for management development?*

genuine situations, and therefore find themselves dealing with real issues. If someone feels underused or not appreciated, it is real and often corresponds to behaviour in the workplace. The difference is that on a course, such processes can be observed and reviewed.

Varying levels of complexity are easily accommodated in MDO programmes. We were once asked to help a freight company which was experiencing resistance to the introduction of a new computer network. There were a number of autonomous freight depots, which, after a delivery, had empty vehicles in another depot's area and would then compete with that depot for business. The new computer system was designed to encourage better usage of vehicles throughout the company and reduce inefficient inter-depot competition, but was perceived as a 'big brother' interference by the managers.

A course was designed with the intention of fostering better relations between the depot managers by helping them to see the folly of internal competition. The crucial exercise set them a task in the outdoors, where teams of managers were set an objective. In a direct reflection of their work attitudes the teams competed fiercely, only realizing afterwards that the common objective had called for co-operation. All readily recognized the parallels with work, and on return made swift improvements which were translated into increased profits for depots and the company as a whole.

Some would argue that outdoor exercises should contain elements of role play or imagination because this adds colour and enhances the memorability, but it is not essential. Indeed it can easily be overdone at the expense of reality. We well remember a senior civil servant running through a wood, pointing his finger and shouting 'Bang, bang!' because his brief had described him as a member of the CIA! With common sense a balance can be found. We have noted that telling a group they cannot touch the ground seems to be more effective than telling them it is a minefield.

Memorability

Any programme or exercise conducted outdoors has huge potential for strong memories: of the experience; the environment; the weather; the learning. This is important: anything that can assist the notoriously fallible human memory is immensely valuable to the trainer.

In MDO, recall of events facilitates recall of learning. A senior management team remember with wry smiles their chairman paddling a rubber dinghy across a river – an amusing and evocative scene – but with that they also remember how it helped them to value all contributions and the importance of them functioning as a team. His complete loss of dignity helped him to recognize that he need not always lead from the front and the importance of using people's skills appropriately.

There are potentially more opportunities for memorable events in the outdoors than in any other area of management development. This is especially so if the exercises include such high-profile outdoor activities as abseiling or cave-exploration. Even run-of-the-mill activities in the company car park contain the potential for long-term recall.

Reduced Barriers to Learning

To most managers the outdoors is an unusual environment. Very few have outdoor skills; and even those such as ex-soldiers, who have some skills, should find that they are of only limited value on a well-designed outdoor programme. Essentially all participants start off on an equal footing.

Because seniority and expertise at the workplace are neutralized, behavioural skills and process awareness become more important. Everyone has something to learn and the outdoors gives them the opportunity to do so.

Even physical fitness should not be a problem. Properly designed exercises should have elements in them which allow everyone to contribute regardless of health, age or fitness. We have seen some quite unfit people successfully attend outdoor programmes.

Shared Experience

Because the outdoor experience is so unusual and absorbing, many delegates – even from disparate backgrounds – build very close bonds of companionship which far outlast the course itself.

If the delegates are from the same company or workplace, the bond will be even stronger and more likely to continue. Early reinforcement of the bonding mechanism by regular and relevant follow-up greatly enhances the process.

This is one reason that outdoor programmes are so popular for teambuilding. It helps people to appreciate each other more, and to understand the value of diversity in teams. If the shared experiences are very memorable, the bonding process can be continually reinforced by recalling the activity, and also by identifying similar situations at work – 'This is just like when we …'

People will not always return from a programme loving each other. They may simply understand each other better. We remember a salesman who commented after a programme that he still didn't like his production manager, but now understood him better and felt he could work with him. This was borne out in their future working relationship which, although never close, was more cordial and much more productive.

The Disadvantages of MDO

These are few and not insuperable, but understanding them will help you to avoid them.

Too Enjoyable

It is quite possible that participants become so wrapped up in enjoying an outdoor exercise that learning is lost. This can largely be overcome by careful facilitation of the review process, helping delegates to recognize the power of the experience as well as the enjoyment.

We sometimes find that teams who overemphasize the enjoyment factor tend also to have problems taking each other seriously at work. The facilitator's role with such teams is to ensure that the learning – which may be painful – is not avoided.

Role Adoption

Some people may overreact to the 'colour' of an exercise and, like the 'CIA' man mentioned earlier, behave abnormally. This has an obviously detrimental effect on the learning process but can be avoided by careful exercise design – and we have found that an exercise is just as valid when played straight as when a spurious storyline is incorporated – and overcome by careful review and feedback.

Denial

Delegates sometimes complain that the exercises are not realistic or are an unfair reflection of their working environment. There are two possible reasons for this:

1. *It is reasonable criticism*: if so, efforts should be made to remedy the situation. It is unhelpful and potentially destructive to learning to ask someone from a particular culture to behave in a way not acceptable in that culture. For example, we once suggested to a coalminer that he use a rock to tap in a tent peg. We thus invited him to break a cardinal safety rule of his industry – only to use tools for the purpose for which they are intended.

2. *As a way of avoiding real issues:* sometimes people use denial ('I wouldn't act like that in real life!') to evade unwelcome truths. This can only be dealt with by careful review.

The Effective Outdoor approach

To summarize, the way to get the best out of MDO is to remember all the points we have considered, maximizing the benefits and minimizing the disadvantages. In particular, ensure that providers understand and use the principles and ethics of experiential learning.

Providers should also be able to design and deliver programmes that address the full learning cycle, taking account of individual learning styles, including:

- exercises which are full of relevant process experience;
- a review of the processes underlying the exercises to articulate the learning that took place;
- input to help delegates to make sense of their learning and put it into a legitimate framework;
- the opportunity for delegates to plan how they will use new ideas in future situations, initially in the next exercise but also on return to work.

ACTIVITY 2

On the request of their instructors, a group of course members on the early hours of an endurance programme disembark from their coach at a remote spot several miles short of its destination. They are told that their dinner is on a nearby island. If they want it, they must swim for it. They are thus given a choice – swim or go hungry. Buoyancy aids are provided, but it is cold.

Consider what the delegates might gain from this and what benefits might accrue to them and their employers. What risks (other than the obvious safety ones, which would be covered by the instructors) are there in such a task?

---

3 The Outdoor Spectrum – Variety, Applications and Styles

▷ SUMMARY ◁

In this chapter we consider the variety of outdoor experiences available.

- We examine the range of outdoor products from the extremely physical through to the lightest of lightweight options. Although categories overlap, we describe four focal points on the outdoor continuum.
- We suggest times when each of the options could be appropriate, and times when they would be inappropriate.

After reading the chapter, you should be able to:

- Understand the variety of physical options available.
- Understand the diverse nature of review options available to you.
- Make an informed and appropriate choice when seeking to resolve a training need through MDO.

Endurance Training

It is perhaps unfortunate that there is a public perception that this rather extreme approach to the outdoors is what MDO is all about. Although sometimes useful, it is only one of several options.

In essence, endurance training is about pushing people to the limit of their physical, psychological, and emotional stamina. Proponents of this approach, which is partly rooted in military-training mythology, claim that by these means delegates discover that they are capable of achieving much more than they believed possible, that they form close emotional bonds with their fellow delegates, and are therefore able to work more effectively together.

This approach to the outdoors can lack subtlety: tasks sometimes require little by way of organization and planning, although they usually demand much by way of sheer physical effort. Classic examples of the genre include forced marches across wild country, ascents of mountains, and wild-water rafting expeditions.

Delegates who have attended such programmes divide into two schools of opinion:

- Those who return from their courses with glowing tributes, having been genuinely and positively touched by their experiences. When asked to state the benefits they talk about having done more than they believed possible, learned how to face challenges, built real comradeship with their compatriots and been emotionally and psychically refreshed.
- Those who find that the level of stress is so great that the experience either has had no effect on relationships and perceptions, or has actually had a negative one.

Applications of Endurance Training for Managers

The benefits of endurance training can be explained relatively simply. First, for most of our lives we are conditioned not to take risks. One day we attend an endurance course and are strongly encouraged to do so. Further, the activities are new and exciting. It comes as no surprise that in these circumstances our energy levels soar, and we rise to the challenges that have been placed all around us.

This does not happen to everyone, but is an observable phenomenon on many endurance programmes. It can be a very good thing – there are great benefits in rediscovering the energy of our earlier years.

Second, the novelty and excitement of the activities is combined with the sudden removal of daily burdens. Family and office cares are left behind, to be replaced by more immediate and clear ones. In terms of the hierarchy of needs (see Figure 3.1 and Maslow (1954)), we are suddenly at the base. The things we have to deal with are immediate, pressing, and simple. This helps build strong and lasting bonds between delegates. As an example, one of the writers attended an endurance course in 1978 and still keeps in touch with his fellow-delegates. He also understands why the generation which fought the Second World War recalls its trials and privations with such relish.

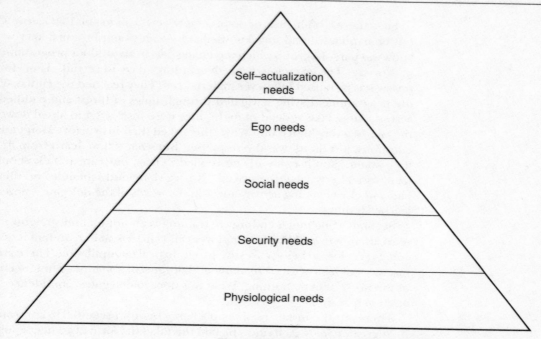

Figure 3.1 *Maslow's hierarchy of needs*

Perhaps the best role that endurance training performs is to provide a peaceful means of building companionship and understanding between people. A kind of war-substitute, in the best sense. Related to this is the role that endurance training can have in teambuilding. When first put together, teams go through a well-remarked phenomenon (see Figure 3.2) known as the forming-storming-norming-performing continuum. This takes time, and can be quite costly because teams are inefficient until they reach the final stage. Anything that hastens the process can therefore save money. Endurance training, through pressure, can hasten the transfer from the forming stage to the storming stage, and hopefully further. Some endurance providers seem to understand this, and we have heard conversations which started 'What can we do to get them shouting at one another?'

Some Concerns

Despite the advantages outlined above, there are some open questions about the approach, and it is characterized by a number of negative factors.

First, there is often little or no process review. This means that learning can be haphazard and unacknowledged. As an example, a manager we know was part of a group which was taking part in an outdoor programme in Norway. The exercises were demanding; days were full. Time for review was promised but never materialized. They reached the climax of the programme: having navigated through miles of forest and paddled across a large lake at dead of night, they were instructed to abseil down the face of a very high dam. 'Why?' they asked their instructor. 'Don't ask questions, just do it!' was the response. 'But what will we learn from it?' they asked. 'You'll enjoy it!' he replied. 'Okay, but can we talk about teamwork afterwards?' they asked. 'No, we're behind schedule.' So they had a week of exciting activity and – in the words of the delegate – never learned a thing.

Second, while much endurance training is an honest and straightforward attempt to build better employees and citizens, at its extremes it can come very close to being excessive psychological manipulation. There are instances of instructors screaming at delegates in a manner reminiscent of the worst military training. What this does to delegates' confidence is open to question.

There are also instances of people being unduly pressured to confront their greatest fears. At its most blatant this takes the form of asking people what they really don't want to do, and then pressuring them into attempting it. It takes little imagination to picture the stress undergone by a young, ambitious manager who happens to have a real fear of enclosed spaces, when goaded into a caving expedition in front of his or her employer. Such things are almost Orwellian in terms of their possible outcome.

There are two risks involved in the 'forming to storming' approach:

- *Failure to transcend the 'storming' phase.* One of the problems with the continuum is that teams can stick at any phase. There is a danger that endurance training takes them as far as storming, and stops there. The result is similar to that achieved by stirring an ants' nest with a stick – a release of energy, conflict, chaos and fury to no particular purpose.
- *Release of the mutiny genie.* Sometimes endurance trainers make outrageous demands which push delegates too far. A natural and healthy response to this – and one which demonstrates laudable independence of mind – is to refuse to co-operate with the trainers, who have no real power to do anything about it. So the lesson of independence and refusal is learned. In some organizations, this may be a dangerous step for delegates' future careers.

Teams don't just spring into active and vibrant life. They tend to go through a process which at times is painful. In brief, the process can be split into four stages:

Forming

Typified by conflict-avoidance. Superficial harmony. Problems often blamed on external factors.

Storming

Frustrations boil over, often causing painful and destructive honesty and real but tactless behaviour (sulking, blaming, and so on). The mirror of 'forming'.

Norming

Group norms and standards emerge. A more mature understanding of each other's strengths and weaknesses also comes about.

Performing

People know each other well enough to get on with the job in an effective way. Personal security is highest in this phase.

This four-stage process, identified by Tuckman (1965) is quite closely related to the life-crisis transition curve, linked to management transitions by Ralph Lewis and Chris Parker (1981). The terms used for the phases of this process coincide neatly with the phase-titles of the team-formation process:

Team formation stages	Transition curve
Forming	Denial
Storming	Blame
Norming	Acceptance
Performing	Development

Figure 3.2 *The team formation process*

So, endurance training has benefits and risks. Summarized, these are:

Benefits	Risks/Limitations
• A greater ability to face challenges.	• Lack of process review.
• The opportunity to create real bonds with fellow delegates.	• Undue physical stress.
• The physical and psychological benefits of time in the mountains away from everyday cares and concerns.	• Psychological manipulation.
	• Can build feelings of inadequacy.
	• Can build false confidence.
• Movement along the 'forming–performing' continuum.	• Can create inter-team disharmony and release the mutiny genie.

Outdoor Education

Also known as adventure training and inaccurately by the generic term 'outward bound', this type of training, while often quite heavily physical, is differentiated from pure 'endurance' programmes in a number of ways:

- The activities are somewhat more complex than the mere survival of a wilderness/mountain/water experience.
- The attitude of trainers is more nurturing and less confronting.
- Some attempt is made to review the activities.
- There is a body of non-military theoretical work underpinning this approach.

Outdoor education is quite a broad church which includes everything from pure outdoor-pursuits providers who occasionally do some outdoor training for managers, through to organizations which are very serious about review, albeit sometimes in a somewhat formulaic manner.

Outdoor education is distinguished from development training in a number of ways:

- Within particular centres, exercises tend to be standardized and do not necessarily focus on particularly relevant management issues.
- Review, while given some value, tends to be less flexible than in development training.

- Although to a lesser degree than in endurance training, exercises are often seen as an end in themselves, rather than a step in the task–do–review cycle.
- Perhaps most importantly, outdoor education stems from a slightly different tradition than development training and its exponents tend to look back at figures from the educational world, such as C. J. Mortlock (1978), rather than to the likes of Herzberg (1959) or Maslow (1954).

Theoretical Background

The original outdoor educationists tended to place great value in the experience in itself. Mortlock talked of 'Peak Experiences', by which he meant those transformational times when, through the meeting of a particular challenge, the completion of a particular task, or the achievement of some outdoor objective, the individual feels uplifted and becomes more aware of the potentialities and opportunities of life. That these moments exist, and that they are greatly beneficial, cannot be denied. Some American educational thinkers, for example, talked of the creation of sixth senses at such times.

The most clear example we know is from a time when we were working with a group of unemployed young-ish people. Most were involved in soft drugs. At the end of a particularly challenging climb, one inveterate drug user sat on a rock, lit a Marlboro, surveyed the peakland scenery and said in tones of thoughtful satisfaction, 'Isn't it good when it's life itself that gives you the highs...' Over the months that followed, outdoor pursuits became part of the route he used to escape from the cycle of unemployment, petty crime and casual drug use which had been his lot for a number of years.

People looking for further examples are referred to the Outward Bound establishment at Eskdale in northwest England where they have commendably preserved dozens of reports from their early days. These are replete with comments from people who found real meaning in life through the challenge of the mountains. Further sources can be found in casual conversations with climbers from Yosemite to the Dolomites.

Applications of Outdoor Education for Managers

There are thousands of examples of outdoor pursuits/adventure education achieving its objectives of building greater self-reliance and self-respect through challenge. That this has clear and useful applications for managers in the late twentieth century is also undeniable:

- Managers undergoing transitions in their working lives can get great value and self-affirmation from outdoor pursuits programmes.
- Managers undergoing stress can benefit from working on challenges of a different kind. A withdrawal from the immediate causes of stress can also improve a person's sense of proportion.
- Sharing outdoor activities with colleagues can help to build real bonds between people. One delegate put it clearly: 'Once you've trusted your life to someone on a cliff face, it's easier to trust them at work.'

There are some questions about the extent of usefulness of outdoor education to the management trainer. These are dealt with in the following section.

Limitations of Outdoor Education for Managers

Outdoor education has its own theoretical background, myths, history and culture. A significant number of excellent management trainers have emerged from it. Yet there is something about the culture that can cause real problems. Why this should be is examined below:

- *Culture clash*: For very good reasons many providers recruit predominantly from the climbing/caving/canoeing worlds. They therefore tend to reproduce the culture of these worlds within their organizations. As an example, the climbing culture is a cheerful, sardonic, anarchic, in-group thing with its own heroes, villains, fashions, morals, controversies and so on. It's fair to say that the average middle-manager is unlikely to have experienced anything like it.

  Problems may arise when there is an interface between cheerfully iconoclastic instructors and groups of managers. It may be that the managers feel that these apparent dropouts can't teach them anything. It may be that the outdoors people see the managers as impossibly anal-retentive and too much of a problem to bother with (we have observed and had to deal with both phenomena), or it may simply be that the groups are too alien to have any meaningful relationship with each other. Whatever the reason, and in whichever direction it happens, there is a real danger of programmes failing through a lack of mutual understanding.
- *Over-identification*: The opposite to the above may occur, and del-

egates may become so besotted with the apparently liberated and fulfilled life of the instructor that they lose heart with their own seemingly humdrum existence and return to work in a far less happy state than when they left it.

- *Clash of value-systems*: Many outdoor education establishments pay their staff incredibly badly. They justify this to their people by pointing out that the work (which might usually be with, for example, inner-city young people) is socially praiseworthy, and provides real non-financial rewards. This is fine until the day that a high-paying management group walks through the door. Staff begin to perceive themselves as having been tricked into low-waged work and the resultant genuine grief can really adversely affect a programme. As one centre director said to us, 'I dread these periodic outbursts of fundamentalism among the staff...'

- *Insufficiently relevant programmes*: Many outdoor education centres have a comfortable and repetitive groove of programmes. This has been called the 'If it's Tuesday it must be canoeing' mentality. When groups of managers appear, they are given the same familiar stuff which may or may not be relevant to their needs. If it isn't, money has been wasted even if delegates enjoy themselves.

- *Ineffective/insufficient process review*. Process review is often important for MDO to be really effective (see Chapter 8). Some outdoor education establishments may be unable to help. One centre head put it to us very clearly: 'The experience is the thing. We don't waste much time on sitting and talking. We like to give a good, full, week.' This is useful for some people, some of the time. It is not useful for all management groups. It really depends on your objectives.

Occasionally, outdoor pursuits centres offer review but quality and quantity can vary wildly. One of the most graphic examples we know occurred to two groups of young employees who, at the end of a week-long programme, participated in a 24-hour exercise. At the end of the exercise one instructor asked his group, 'Did you enjoy yourselves?' 'Yes' they replied, and that was the end of the review! Meanwhile another group were embarking on what was to become a two-hour review.

The problem is that an experience-focused provider sees review as of secondary importance. The energy – and the focus – of outdoor pursuits providers is often on experience rather than analysis. This can lead to patchy or even non-existent review.

Summarized, the benefits and risks of outdoor education are as follows:

Benefits	Risks/limitations
• Can build greater self-esteem.	• Culture/value clash.
• Can help people in transition.	• Over-identification.
• Can help relieve stress.	• Irrelevance of programmes.
• Can build close bonds between colleagues.	• Lack of process review.

Development Training

Like outdoor education, development training covers a broad spectrum of training methods. Our definition of the term – a personal one– is *the application of outdoor solutions to personal and group development needs, ensuring that the major focus of programmes is on meeting particular and stated aims.*

In our view, this definition also gives hints as to the difference between outdoor education and development training. In the former, the experience – particularly the 'peak experience' – is paramount. In the latter, the experience is merely a means to some pre-stated end and so the focus is much more on review. The difference is summarized below:

Outdoor education	Development training
Focuses on the experience.	Focuses on the human processes which underlie the experience.
Sees the outdoors as an end in itself.	Sees the outdoors as the means to an end.
Often does not place much emphasis on process review.	Places heavy emphasis on process review
Recruits predominantly from the outdoor world.	Recruits from outdoor, industrial training, and psychological worlds.
Is often limited to areas where there is an abundance of outdoor media – cliffs, caves and the like – available.	Often occurs in mountainous/watery areas, but can take place anywhere, even including city centres.
Puts emphasis on doing.	Puts emphasis on reflecting and resolving.

Evolving separately but similarly in Britain and America, out of a marriage of outdoor pursuits and 'indoor' management development in the late 1970s, development training has become something different from, but still with elements of, both. It arose in the 1970s out of a challenging of traditional outdoor methods which originally found expression in a number of ways which are discussed in Chapter 1.

Characteristics of Development Training

Several things distinguish development training from its near neighbours:

- *Clear and particular process objectives*: Development programmes start with the identification of clear process objectives. These depend on the needs of the client. We examine the most frequent in Chapter 4. In some cases a need might be common enough to provide an open programme; many development training organizations concentrate on these common areas. On the other hand some providers offer programmes tailored to the needs of particular clients.

- *Emphasis on review*: Development trainers often see the exercise merely as a means of generating process. This process is then reviewed in post-exercise (or mid-exercise on longer tasks) sessions. There are a wide variety of process review methods used. These are discussed in Chapter 8. It is sufficient at this point to draw your attention to Figure 1.3 which points out the differences between process and task review.

  Proponents of development training claim that process review is the whole point of exercises, and that it is in review that the real learning takes place. Our own experience is that this is true for those people who like to reflect before arriving at conclusions. Other people arrive at conclusions during exercises; to this latter group review is more important as a way of communicating their learning to others.

- *Specially designed exercises*: If clear objectives have been identified, it follows that exercises must enable the wished-for processes to occur. Most providers of development training therefore find themselves designing new or variant exercises quite frequently.

- *Encompassing a range of physicality*: The level of physicality varies from one provider to another, and even from one programme to another. Nevertheless with some overlap the overall range is less physical than in outdoor education, if only because the pauses for review allow the body to recover.

- *Review is supplemented*: Although this happens to a greater or lesser extent in other areas of MDO, development trainers customarily use such things as psychometrics, other questionnaires, and inputs of relevant theory to reinforce the messages of experience. Sometimes it's done well and helps delegates to make sense of their experiences; sometimes it's done badly, as when trainers tell delegates what they are supposed to have learned... Nevertheless, supplements to the do/review cycle are a hallmark of development training.

Benefits of Development Training for Managers

Development training has wide applications in management training. We deal with these in some detail in Chapter 4. It is sufficient to say here that the best development training, particularly when tailored to the needs and cultures of particular client-groups, can have a very powerful impact on managers' development. For a wide variety of reasons this does not always hold true, but even short, sharp programmes can see significant progress in team and manager-development.

The benefits of development training are as follows:

- *Process reality*: Because development training reproduces and sometimes amplifies the stresses and strains of working processes, delegates often behave as they do at work. This gives the delegates, as well as their trainers and counsellors, the opportunity to see how they perform, see their reactions to stress and pressure, and consider alternative reactions.
- *Experimental approaches*: Again because workplace stresses are reproduced and amplified in a different situation, delegates can experiment with different approaches to management, perhaps finding one that is more appropriate to them and their situation. Such experimentation at the workplace might cost much more in terms of both self-esteem and hard cash.
- *Ability to review situations*: A phenomenon arising out of review is the realization that at work, too, it is possible to review and learn from mistakes. One delegate put it neatly for us: 'All I've learned is to stand back and think after I've done a job, as well as before... for me, that is enough...'
- *Helps people in transition*: By reproducing situations in which newly promoted managers (for example) find themselves, the managers

are able to learn to cope with those situations more readily at work. In effect, good development training helps people to manage the transition curve (see Figure 3.2).

- *An effective substitute for other experience:* Dr Valerie Stewart (Stewart and Stewart (1978))once said that all training should include at least surrogate experience. Good development training goes further – the experience, although not usually task-realistic as far as working life is concerned, is very process-real. Experience gained on a development programme is very transferable.

- *Can be a catalyst for a major review of approaches to life and work:* In the mid-seventies one of the authors attended an experimental encounter group, and was impressed by the way the programme got to the root of people's problems. Perhaps it's coincidence, but several of the delegates (himself included) moved into more fulfilling careers in the following years. There was a 'down' side – several of the delegates experienced very real pain from exposing areas of their personality that they would much rather have kept concealed.

We were attracted to development training because it had the capacity to get to the root of problems without the same psychological pain being evident. Certainly, we have seen people radically reappraise their approach to life and work during development programmes. Follow-up suggests that these changes can stick.

Limitations of Development Training for Managers

Despite its undoubted power and manager-friendliness, development training has its limitations. These can be seen as a lack of applicability to organizational problems and a failure to meet physical expectations.

Applicability to organizational problems

Although development training is undoubtedly a flexible medium, it is appropriate for working on human rather than organizational issues in businesses. Sometimes apparently organizational problems actually contain a major human element (see Appendix 3 on p. 130). Purely structural problems, however, cannot be successfully addressed using MDO, but MDO can be a helpful *contribution* when combined with the right structural initiatives.

The worst programme we ever ran was one in which the problems turned out not to be with the delegates, but with the organizational structure. For political reasons two departments whose work overlapped heavily were kept separate and under different senior managers, with duplicated functions everywhere and demarcation disputes and cross-blaming happening all the time. It was perceived by the senior managers that the problem was one of lack of understanding between their respective junior managers and supervisors.

We were called in and ran a joint programme that emphasized the need for co-operation. Instead of this being the revelation we had expected, the staffs co-operated willingly – just as they had always done at work, albeit secretly. This left us with a thoroughly inappropriate programme which, despite our attempts to make it more relevant, was a lost cause. The real problem was organizational – there was really no need for the two departments. Given the opportunity, the people wanted to co-operate.

While not useful for solving purely organizational problems, development training works very well when addressing human reactions to organizational problems. An illustrative example is the case of the large engineering company which, having sensibly reorganized, found that its middle managers had failed to accept the reorganization, and were behaving as if nothing had happened.

A development training programme was organized in which, through an outdoor business game, they were given the opportunity to work within both the old and the new forms of organization. It rapidly became clear that the old was less efficient and more frustrating than the new. A full acceptance of the reorganization followed. The old Confucian saying, 'I hear, I forget; I see, I remember; I do, I understand' could be expanded to 'I am told, I reject; I do, I understand; I feel, I accept.'

Meeting expectations

Most outdoor providers, including development trainers, emphasize the outdoor element of their programmes in their publicity material. The media do likewise. The conventional wisdom is that no-one is excited by pictures of reviews, so show them pictures of people doing dangerous-looking things with ropes, rocks, and rafts.

The effect of all this machismo PR is that sometimes delegates expect – and look forward to – a really heavy programme of intense physical stress and pressure-bonding. When they find that much of their time is being spent reflecting on and discussing their actions, they feel cheated. It is as well to brief participants on what to expect before they arrive on programmes.

As with the other classifications, development training has benefits and limitations. Summarized, these are:

Benefits
- Process reality.
- Allows experimentation with managerial methods.
- Imparts the ability to review situations.
- Helps people in transition.
- An effective experience-substitute.
- A catalyst for change.

Limitations
- Not applicable to organizational (as opposed to human) problems.
- Can fail to meet physical expectations.

Lightweight Programmes

In addition to the three major categories listed above, there is a growing trend (in which the authors are participating) towards physically lighter-weight programmes where there is an admixture of outdoor exercises with indoor experiential ones. This has several advantages:

- *Perceived low physicality*: Some managers fear the apparent levels of physical stress on programmes which espouse heavy exertion, and are happier with the lighter option.
- *Ability to operate in non-mountainous areas*: A client put it to us very clearly: 'These other people wanted us to spend two whole days travelling. You just came to the company sports field with some scaffolding and wood, and off we went...' Management time is expensive. Why waste it in travel?
- *A clearer emphasis on process*: Sometimes all the accoutrements of the outdoors – Karabiners, wet suits, caving lamps – can become so engrossing to delegates that even on the most process-dedicated programmes they interfere with group process. An analogy is the way that a fascination with the technology of video can sometimes spoil presentation programmes.

A disadvantage of the lighter-weight approach is that the programmes may have less of a sense of occasion about them than the full outdoor event. This may well have a knock-on effect on learning. It may also be seen as a cheap substitute.

Outdoor Inputs in Indoor Programmes

As the outdoors has become more accepted as a legitimate medium for management training, there has been a trend to include short outdoor inputs – usually one day – into predominantly indoor programmes.

At its best this is a very good thing: it enables delegates to practise new ways of doing things before they return to work and also gives the pragmatist/activists (see Chapter 2) an opportunity to reinforce their learning while giving everyone a time of reflection away from the pressures of the group room.

There are some problems with the one-day input. One day is too short a time to deal with in-depth process issues, and thus there is a temptation for trainers to keep it sweet and shallow. Because of this lack of penetration, delegates can see it as a 'play-day', which is very good at one level but usually not what clients and trainers really want. At its worst it is just a way of padding the programme. This, however, applies to any training if done badly.

KEY:

VH = VERY HIGH; H = HIGH;
M = MEDIUM; L = LOW; VL = VERY LOW.

Hyphenated letters (e.g L-H) denote a range within the style.

	Endurance	Adventure	Development	Lightweight	Contribution
PHYSICALITY	VH	H	M-H	L-M	L-M
COMPLEXITY	L	L-M	M-H	M-H	L-M
FOCUSED DESIGN	L	L	H	H	L
PROCESS REVIEW	VL	L-M	M-H	M-H	L-H

Figure 3.3 *The outdoor spectrum summarized*

ACTIVITY 3

Having arrived at an outdoor pursuits centre the previous day, and having spent their time since arrival on a variety of lightweight tasks of around an hour's duration each, a group of managers and supervisors (varying ages, weights and sexes) are taken to a clifftop and given a short but sufficient input on abseiling techniques. They are then invited to do some abseiling, with instructors acting as safety and 'belay' people.

Consider what the individuals and group might gain from this, and what benefits might accrue to them and their employers. What risks (other than the obvious safety ones, which would be covered by the instructors) are there in such a task?

4

The Outdoor Industry – Growth, Uses and Limitations

▷   SUMMARY   ◁

In this chapter:

- We study the growth of MDO, with an examination and categorization of providers.
- We make suggestions for times when the outdoors is a good way of meeting training needs, examining some successful applications.
- We suggest areas where it may be inappropriate to use the outdoors, again illustrating with examples.

After reading this chapter, you should:

- Understand the provider options available to you.
- Know when the outdoors is a good option to pursue in meeting your training needs.
- Know when to consider other options first.

The Outdoor Industry

When we first discussed this book, we considered calling it *The Exploding Mountain*. This was not simply to attract attention, but also because we thought it an accurate reflection of the way in which the MDO business has mushroomed since the mid-1970s.

As late as 1983, a generally excellent encyclopaedia of management development techniques could only manage half a page on the outdoors (as compared to a similar or greater amount on such techniques as

Parrainage, Crossover Groups, and Socratic Enquiry!) If the same encyclopaedia was written today, we are sure that considerably more space
would be needed merely to list the best-known suppliers.

We have examined the evolution of MDO in Chapter 1 and the range
of philosophies in Chapter 3. This section deals with the range of enter-
prises now available to the buyer, and reasons for using particular ones. A
simple chart for comparing suppliers is also included (Figure 4.2).

The range can be categorized in a number of ways:

- accommodation;
- range of outdoor media;
- exercise design skills;
- review skills; and
- flexibility of provision, of design and of location.

We shall consider these in turn.

Accommodation

In the late 1970s, only extremes of accommodation were available: either
outdoor centres with dormitories and institutional food or hotels with
gourmet menus and an inbuilt belief that they were hosting corporate
incentive programmes which really wanted two-hour dinners every night.

Times have changed since then, and a much fuller range is available.
Many outdoor centres have invested in better sleeping accommodation
and a wider range of menu options; some have gone as far as providing
purpose-designed management accommodation away from the main
building with specialist catering and single bedrooms. Hotels have also
woken up to the needs of MDO clients, and flexible service is now readily
available.

In addition there are now a number of development training venues
specifically aimed at attracting management business, with a wide range
of comfort levels. We know of some which are just above institutional
level, and others with a real bias towards managers, with good group
rooms and excellent and appropriate food.

As far as use is concerned, the key question before booking accommodation is 'What suits the group best?' Foolish though it seems, inappropriate accommodation can cause (or be used to create) real problems to
groups in accepting the training. This is particularly true of centres where
the regime is geared to the needs of young people and school groups.
Other questions worth considering are:

- *Adaptability*: For example, does the centre provide sufficiently
varied catering? Do staff work inflexible hours?

- *Appropriateness*: Is the comfort level high enough not to cause distractions? Is it too high – do people have to dress up for dinner?
- *Suitable regime*: Are centre staff accustomed to working with adults? Is a management group going to cause culture shock?

Range of Outdoor Media

The best outdoor programmes are often those in which a variety of outdoor media are utilized. Programmes containing an overwhelming amount of one particular medium can become quite boring for participants. It is therefore wise to investigate what media the provider uses. A list is included in Figure 4.1, below

Rock-face activities Climbing Abseiling Mountain rescue Other	**Navigational Tasks** Expeditions – wild country Expeditions – low level Orienteering – wild country Orienteering – low level Other
Underground activities Caving Cave surveying Mine exploration Other	**Grounds activities** Simple 'box 1' tasks (eg 2m wall). Medium–complex box 2/3 tasks (eg various 'across the gap' tasks) Interactive but not 'exposing' tasks (eg low-level ropes courses) Passive but 'exposing' (eg aerial runways) Interactive but 'exposing' (eg 'high ropes' tasks) Larger grounds-based tasks (eg bridge-building, etc)
Water-based activities Raft building Open canoeing (still water) Kayak work (still water) Kayak work (wild water) Kayak work (sea) Dinghy sailing Larger vessels Other water-based	**Other media** (eg non-outdoor experiential tasks)

Figure 4.1 *The range of outdoor media*

Exercise Design Skills

The growth in the number of outdoor providers does not seem to have been matched by a real growth in the number of exercises available for MDO. There are a variety of reasons for this.

First, there are only a few outdoor media, and many providers tend to use these unimaginatively. This leads to the 'Monday Climbing, Tuesday Sailing' mentality. Second, some providers see risks in moving away from the tried-and-trusted, so tend to use repetitively a number of old favourites. This is particularly true of some established providers, who have become very bureaucratic. It can take months to pioneer a new exercise in these circumstances, and even the most innovative of employees often give up the struggle and relax into the old patterns. Third, some providers of MDO are so busy that no-one has time to do anything other than tasks well known to all.

At the other extreme, we know of some providers who seek change at any price, and are constantly modifying exercises and programmes, seeking continuing novelty. The results can be extremely unpredictable and dark tales are told of rogue courses ending in arrest for delegates.

Between the extremes there is a whole spectrum, catering to a very wide range of needs. Some organizations straddle large parts of that spectrum; others are clearly marooned at a particular point on it. Our advice to purchasers is to find suppliers who match their own culture – they are much more likely to understand it, and the choice is wide.

Review Skills

While most people involved in MDO *say* that review is important, the range of skill and thus the actual level of ability in this area is extremely wide. Listening to the assurances of suppliers' representatives is no guarantee of review skills. A word with their clients often provides a better insight into an organization's review methods. If this is impracticable, answers to the following questions can be helpful:

- *How do your people learn review skills?* If there is no clear answer, then at best they pick it up as they go along. At worst there is no review.
- *How often are their review skills appraised, and how?* If someone has bluffed their way through the first question, this will expose the bluff. If you still have doubts, then a third question will clarify their real attitude to review.
- *What do you/they consider to be the three most important skills in review?* Answers can vary, and different people give different but perfectly valid responses. What is interesting is the level at which they are pitched. This can be very revealing of their understanding of the depth of the review process. For the record, our particular answer (in no special order) is:
    1. The ability to listen and not betray feelings by facial expression.

2. The ability to formulate the right open/probing questions.
3. The ability to create conditions in which process emerges from the group.

There are always extremes, and over-reviewing is as dangerous as under-review. We know of cases where groups have disintegrated because a trainer was obsessed with the need to review every gesture and intonation.

Flexibility of Provision

While many providers of MDO are very flexible, factors such as innate conservatism can lead to inflexibility on the part of a minority.

An extreme example is the trainer who, having designed a programme in the late 1970s is *still* running it without deviating in the slightest degree. The old saw 'If it ain't broke, don't fix it!' is of course true but the world has changed a lot since 1978, and programmes should always reflect the real world.

Another form of inflexibility is demonstrated by those providers who become hostage to a particular technique, seeing everything in its terms. Programme content should always be dictated by client needs, not fashion or fanaticism.

Several organizations have discovered this to their cost, an example being the centre which had a training team so infatuated with Transactional Analysis and its derivatives that all courses, whatever their objectives, turned into very intense analyses.

The times dictated that the bulk of the clients were young and unemployed, and it was tragic to see the mutual frustration which developed between trainers (keen to explore the furthest recesses of post-Freudian analysis) and trainees (keen to discover some area in which they could legitimately gain some self-esteem). The deadlock was only broken when a very predictable shortage of business led to most of the training team being made redundant.

Flexibility of Design

The range of MDO programmes has become so wide that it could be argued that flexibility of design is unnecessary, having been supplanted by flexibility of supply.

Nevertheless, there are occasions when it is wise to build a long-term relationship with one supplier. In these circumstances, purchasers should ensure that they choose one who is able to provide the range of programmes they require.

Accommodation:	Unsuitable	1	2	3	4	5	Suitable
Range of Media:	Very low	1	2	3	4	5	Very high
Design Ability:	Very low	1	2	3	4	5	Very high
Review Skills:	Very low	1	2	3	4	5	Very high
Flexibility							
of provision:	Very low	1	2	3	4	5	Very high
of design:	Very low	1	2	3	4	5	Very high
of location:	Very low	1	2	3	4	5	Very high

In all cases, circle the appropriate number, with 1 being low quality and 5 being high quality. A slight exception to this is the item on accommodation, when you must first decide what you prefer, and then mark accordingly.

Although simple, the chart should help buyers of training to decide between providers or, at least, highlight problem areas.

Figure 4.2 *Chart for comparing suppliers*

Some providers have an excellent reputation for work with young people but are ineffective with management groups; others are specialists in senior management and expensively ineffective with graduate groups. Investigation pays dividends.

Flexibility of Location

One of the real benefits to arise from the growth of MDO in the last ten years is the emergence of a number of fully equipped MDO organizations unlinked to any fixed centre or even geographical district.

By necessity these organizations have been at the forefront of new initiatives in MDO, literally taking it to the most unlikely places and exercising considerable ingenuity in running outdoor programmes in even the most urban of environments.

The benefits to clients of this flexible approach are numerous. Principal among them are:

- *Adaptable provision of training*: Because they exist by providing training where the client wants it, the mobile providers have become adept at quickly designing and resourcing exercises to meet a wide variety of needs.

- *Adaptable location and accommodation*: Mobile organizations are able to provide a wide range of accommodation options to meet the varied training and financial circumstances of their clients.

The flexibility of the mobile providers has positively affected many of the better fixed suppliers, even leading to some adding an in-company service. Nevertheless, mobile organizations continue to lead the way in providing, for example, international and multi-national training.

In Figure 4.2, we set out a table which can be used by suppliers and purchasers. Suppliers can use it as a way of analysing their service in a detached manner. Purchasers of MDO can use it to compare suppliers, helping them to sort out the one they need from the bewildering variety available.

Using the Outdoors

In Chapter 2 we discussed why MDO is such a powerful learning medium and pointed out some of the potential disadvantages. We also emphasized that MDO is a medium, not a message in itself. There are some learning objectives for which MDO is particularly suitable and some where it is not. Our aim here is to examine some of the objectives for which MDO is more commonly used and some examples of how they have been addressed.

Our own view is that MDO is sometimes restricted by being too tightly focused to narrow subject-headed learning objectives. Its most potent use is as a tool of organization development, enabling people to feel the real benefits and stresses of a particular organizational change, and encouraging cultural flexibility. An example of this application of MDO is set out in Appendix 3.

Despite its usefulness and flexibility as an OD tool, MDO is most often used for a variety of particular training applications of which a comprehensive, but by no means exhaustive, list is included in Figure 4.3. We will examine in detail some of the more common areas including:

- Teambuilding,
- Problem solving and decision making,
- Creativity,
- Leadership,
- Behaviour changes.

- Leadership training
- Team development
- Personal control
- Improving communications
- Encouraging creativity
- Stress management
- Interpersonal skills
- Change management
- Planning
- Decision making
- Project management

Figure 4.3 *Some applications of MDO*

Teambuilding

The most common and popular reason for choosing MDO is team-building (an example is outlined in Figure 4.4). Often, established teams recognize the value of playing together to help them work better together. Some teams regularly socialize, with or without partners, some play golf, some chase each other with paint guns.

Any of these activities can help the team development process. However, the real key to getting the maximum benefit from such activities is in careful, structured review. This may not be appropriate after a round of golf or a dinner dance, but is a crucial part of any good development programme.

To focus on building the team, the programme needs to involve the whole team, in both the exercises and the review. If the team is large, it may be necessary to work in sub-groups for part of the programme to allow maximum involvement. However, there should be at least one exercise where the whole group is interacting in a genuinely non-competitive way to pull the team together.

Time and consideration should always be given to any team member who, for whatever reason, does not attend the programme. Teambuilding which excludes any team member, even a peripheral one, can initiate or exacerbate elitism or isolation, which can be very destructive and negate the gains from a programme.

The team should, with help if necessary, recognize and discuss the issue before returning and agree a clear strategy for integrating others into the team. This may include:

Teambuilding
A well known and successful consultancy, specializing in Total Quality Management, recognized a weakness in the training they provided to their clients. The TQM principles were encapsulated in a three-pronged approach of systems, control and teamwork and they had a wealth of experience and expertise in the first two.

They were concerned, however, that they only had a superficial understanding of teamwork.* They therefore asked us to design and facilitate a one-day seminar with their senior consultants. The day was run from their offices, but the activities ranged into the neighbouring public park.

Combined with some psychometric analysis of potential team strengths we ran a number of short problem-solving exercises and a carefully adapted version of the 'Riotous Assembly' exercise described in Figure 7.6.

The ensuing review was wide ranging, but also quite deep in certain aspects. The consultants found a number of areas where they felt a need to improve their own working relationships and structure, which in turn gave them a greater understanding of the importance of the teamwork part of their programmes and some fresh ideas on how to impart the message.

Some recent surveys in Europe have shown that as many as 80 per cent of TQM initiatives fail. Part of the reason for this is neglect of the teamwork training process (Kearney 1991).

Figure 4.4 *Example 1 – Teambuilding*

- describing experiences;
- sharing learning;
- explaining planned changes;
- inviting and listening to their comments;
- adjusting plans to involve them and incorporate their ideas;
- giving them a clear role in feedback on changes and their effect.

The ideal situation is to involve everybody from the beginning. It is important to measure the cost of taking everybody against the *true* cost of leaving someone behind.

Creativity
A company that prided itself on quality and customer service recognized a change in customers' expectations and requirements. The company was increasingly being asked to design innovative marketing ideas, rather than just manufacture products.

During a teambuilding programme the delegates struggled with a series of problem-solving exercises, which during review was blamed on a lack of innovative thought. This seemed to be backed up by the results of the Belbin Team Roles profiles, which identified only one 'plant' (innovator) in a group of 88 middle and senior managers. (She was subsequently sacked!)

The initial reaction to this was to advocate recruitment of more innovative types. However we recommended they spend some time considering their culture first. Their reputation was built on some fairly inflexible systems and a culture of compliance and tradition, which fostered intolerance of new ideas.

We ran a series of programmes to encourage more creativity and, more importantly, to recognize and appreciate innovation and the need for it.

Figure 4.5 *Example 2 – Creativity*

Problem Solving and Decision Making

These associated skills are rightly valued in business and often identified as a major training need. They are helped by adopting a structured approach, such as suggested in Chapter 6. In fact it is often necessary to introduce this model on a programme regardless of objectives as poor problem solving can contribute to poor performance in exercises and slow down the learning process.

To evaluate this structured approach fully, a variety of exercises is required, reflecting the different situations or boxes described in the Williams–Creswick window, Figure 7.1 (p 90). The solution will be obvious to some, to others less so. In some exercises the whole solution will be identified at once, in others it will only emerge towards the end, as a series of separate, but connected, problems are dealt with sequentially. Some exercises will have similar solutions or draw on the experience of earlier problems, just as problems at work are often similar and managers can apply lessons from the past.

Having introduced and practised a structured approach, it may be necessary to spend time emphasizing the potential limitations of too much structure, which may inhibit innovation and stall the problem-solving process – this is examined more fully in the next section.

Creativity

It has been said and is largely true that creativity cannot be taught. However, it can be encouraged and developed. Many individuals and organizations are not considered very creative. They may *be* very creative, but have developed with or within a very tight structure, which inhibits creative thought.

Although structure and clear limits are important, particularly in business, they can become a hindrance if too rigid. The real learning in a creativity programme is in recognizing the need and ability to challenge and work outside limits (see Figure 4.5).

The outdoor medium is an alien environment and helps people to examine assumptions and to work 'outside the box.' There is scope to provide problem-solving exercises which encourage creative solutions. It is important that such exercises have broad constraints, a number of possible answers and the trainers are prepared for and receptive to unexpected solutions.

Crucial, though, to success is the transfer of learning back to work. Delegates must recognize that the freedom to experiment and be innovative is not peculiar to the outdoors, and realize its benefits in the working environment.

Leadership

As we indicated in Chapter 1, one of the roots of MDO was the use by the military of short practical exercises, WOSBs, to test and evaluate leadership potential in aspirant officers. Unfortunately these exercises were not reviewed with the participants, only by the observing, evaluating officers.

Later in military training similar exercises are sometimes used, where the appointed leader is debriefed and occasionally asked for his/her own comments. However, the feedback tends to be quite critical and is nearly always focused on the task, with little thought given to the feelings of the team or individuals in it.

Here lies the fundamental difference in the good MDO approach. All team members should be involved in the review process and the facilitator will avoid judging performance or prescribing improvements.

Leadership

Some National Health Service managers were trying to come to terms with their new roles in the market environment introduced by the government. In particular they were concerned about the apparently conflicting functions of providing and purchasing health care for their clients – the patients. We designed and ran a large multi-task exercise where managers had to bid for contracts, buy tasks to fulfil those contracts and then complete the tasks. The tasks themselves varied from simple, repetitive operations with low value to longer problem-solving exercises of high value to further reflect the conflicting priorities of their hospital environments. This proved to be a reasonable allegory and the managers developed a number of strategies which they successfully adapted to their real situations and transferred to their new Health Trusts.

Figure 4.6 *Example 3 – Leadership*

Instead of telling the leader 'You should have…', they will ask 'How could you have…?'

A leadership programme will give as many opportunities as possible for delegates to take a leadership role. Some exercises will contain several such roles, possibly with subordinate leaders. Another useful device to maximize leadership chances is to run a larger exercise in phases. This provides useful breaks for review and valuable lessons in information transfer.

This is not to say that delegates only learn during 'their turn'; there is as much learning in being led and in recognizing the importance of good 'followership' – no leader can do it all!

Specific Behaviour Changes

The world is experiencing constant and accelerating change, and when changes in organization, market forces or customer expectations necessitate a new approach or a change in management behaviour, MDO can provide a safe and supervised medium in which to test and practise the new behaviours or skills. Exercises can be designed which are metaphors of the changed world, enabling delegates to experiment in finding appropriate ways of managing (see Figure 4.6).

When to Choose Another Option

Training purchasers can become as enthusiastic about MDO as providers. While this is often a happy situation, it can lead to inappropriate courses and disillusioned trainees, and in turn unhappy purchasers.

While creative providers can produce exercises or programmes to address practically any training need and less creative, but persuasive, providers can convince of the suitability of MDO for any need, it should always be remembered that it is in the interest of providers to find new uses for the medium.

- It was successful or popular last time.
- It is cheaper than the other options.
- It worked for our competitors.
- It will be a nice change, a bit of a reward for the troops.
- It will toughen them up, sort out the men from the boys.
- We all had to go through it.
- It is part of the package the supplier provides.
- It will make me look progressive.

Figure 4.7 *Wrong reasons to choose MDO*

For the training manager it is more important to consider whether MDO is the *best* vehicle to achieve the objectives. We include a short list at Figure 4.7 of spurious reasons for choosing MDO as a training solution. If any of these arguments are being used, *think again*.

In this section we consider some examples of where outdoor programmes are not the answer to training or development problems.

Incidental Helpfulness

Because of the reality of MDO experiences, many management skills contribute to success or failure and emerge in review. These are perfectly valid and should be addressed, but only on 'open' personal development programmes could they be considered central items. Such areas include:

- assertiveness;
- time management;
- influencing and persuading skills;
- customer service; and
- quality assurance.

Others can easily be built into a course, but would not be ideal primary objectives, such as:

- presentation skills;
- meeting skills; or
- delegation.

When MDO is a waste of time and money

MDO can do a lot of things, being exceptionally useful as a way of developing people and teams, and being an excellent organizational development tool enabling people to come to terms with, and experiment upon, ways of coping in new organizations and situations.

Only rarely – and then only if people with sufficient power in the organization are present – can MDO cope with basic structural faults in organizations. On our 'worst ever' course, referred to on p 47, we were assured by company training staff and senior managers that the delegates (from two separate but closely related departments) heartily disliked each other and needed to learn to work together.

It soon became clear that the delegates actually got on exceptionally well, and that the real problems were structural; the departments actually needed to merge. As our programme had been carefully designed to highlight the futility of conflict as opposed to co-operation, and as people already were co-operating, we struggled to make the programme work.

The reason for the departments remaining separate was quite simple: the two department heads (not present on the programme) had too much to lose, and refused to countenance an otherwise obvious organizational need, seeking instead to divert blame on to their 'uncooperative' subordinates.

ACTIVITY 4

A group of 12 managers (mixed age, sex and physical ability) is taken to a rock face. Here they are handed a written brief that tells them they have two-and-a-half hours to set up and operate a factory, the products of which will be abseils (downward) and mountain-rescue hauls (upward). There are cash benefits for each completed 'unit' of haul-and-abseil, and cash costs for hire of equipment over the basic minimum for safety.

All the delegates have received training on use of the backup safety rope, and half have received haulage training and half abseiling training. No-one has received both abseiling and haulage training. The role of the instructors is limited to observing for safety problems (and intervening should any arise), setting and securing the appropriate slings and belays, and – for a fee – answering technical questions.

There is enough equipment to set up two production lines.

Consider what the individuals and group might gain from this task, and what benefits might accrue to them and their employers. What issues might arise that need to be reviewed? How might these relate to issues in a real factory? What risks (other than the safety ones, which would be covered by the instructors) are there in this task?

5 The Role of Clients' Training Staff

▷ SUMMARY ◁

In this chapter we discuss how the company training specialist can enhance and improve the effectiveness of an MDO programme.

- We suggest regular liaison with the supplier.
- We detail how to fully prepare delegates for the course.
- We show how a company trainer can use MDO 'in-house'.

After reading the chapter you should be able to:

- Ensure the best service from the provider.
- Help delegates to gain the maximum benefit from a course.
- Design and run your own exercises.

Having decided that MDO is the appropriate medium, and having chosen a supplier and decided upon a programme, there is still much a client's training specialist can do to ensure that maximum benefit is gained from the programme. These considerations include:

- Liaison with the provider throughout the process.
- Briefing and preparation of delegates.
- Follow up training and evaluation.

In addition, we will examine ways in which MDO can be integrated into an organization's internal programmes without resort to specialist providers.

Liaison with Providers

The closer and more frequent the contact and co-operation between the company trainer and the supplier, the better the results of a programme. Objectives of these regular contacts will include:

- *Ensuring that programme objectives are fully understood by all involved in design and delivery*: Failure in either of these areas is a guarantee of wasted money. The result will be an unfocused general development effort, satisfying few.
- *Monitoring progress of design and preparation*: Organizations employ training staff to ensure that they get value for money. Some interpret this as trying to obtain a five percent reduction in guest tutors' travelling expenses. More sensible ones check progress with suppliers, asking for outline programmes (with explanations) well in advance of the course date. This allows sufficient time for any modifications that may be required.
- *Checking relevance and appropriateness of planned exercises and reviews*: See above.
- *Involvement in delivery*: Many client staff trainers are taken in by the mystique with which some suppliers' trainers surround themselves. It is actually extremely useful for trainers from the client organization to be involved in delivery of MDO programmes as they can add unique understanding of in-company problems which might well not be obvious to outsiders, no matter how well briefed.
- *Visiting the programme*: At the very least, clients' training specialists should visit programmes. Nothing gives more of a flavour of a programme than actual experience of the atmosphere.
- *Seeking suppliers' perceptions of the extent to which objectives were met*: Suppliers are usually keen to do a good job, and to give a professional service. Given this, it is surprising how few clients seek feedback on the extent to which general programme objectives were met.

Preparation of Delegates

Delegates usually benefit most from courses for which they have been adequately prepared. They should be involved from as early as possible in the process, knowing what is envisaged and why.

The organization's training staff should ensure that delegates know and understand the course objectives and have considered, preferably in discussion with their direct superior, how objectives apply to them. Areas of personal need and development should also be discussed and ways in which the programme addresses these identified. If delegates are attending as a result of a need identified at appraisal, this should be made clear to them.

Many people feel quite natural fears before attending an outdoor programme. This is for a variety of reasons, including:

- Misplaced humour from colleagues – sad, but some people find it killingly funny to regale potential delegates with tales of frozen nights spent on mountain tops in plastic sacks…
- Genuine fear provoked by media images of MDO, which tend to focus on the nastiest bits of the most physical programmes.
- Unhappy memories of school outdoor pursuits weekends.

A meeting of potential delegates several weeks before the course is a very worthwhile investment, as fears can be addressed and dealt with, expectations can be shared, and domestic and logistic fears put to rest (people need to know what type of clothes to bring, what will be provided, levels of privacy, and so on). Such a meeting should involve both the organization's and the supplier's staff. As well as the above, the meeting can be used to:

- introduce the supplier's staff;
- introduce delegates to each other, saving valuable course time;
- address any unrealistic hopes;
- confirm administrative arrangements;
- explain the course methods; and ·
- invite and encourage delegates to obtain the maximum benefit from the opportunities of the course. Some suggestions for delegates are included in Figure 5.1.

Follow Up

Planning for the delegates' reception on their return is as important as thoroughly preparing them beforehand. Many a good programme has been devalued by the attitudes of delegates' colleagues on return to work. We know of one case where a very senior manager actually said, 'The holiday's over now – get back to work!' to a middle manager who was returning (full of ideas) from an outdoor programme. Client-organizations' trainers should work to ensure a sympathetic and constructive dialogue between returning delegates, their managers and peers.

1. Clarify personal objectives. These may not be the same as the company's. Reconcile management learning objectives with personal ones, such as desire to abseil or enter a cave, and prioritize them.
2. Discuss objectives with management, training department, colleagues, family and friends – anyone who can provide objectivity, support or criticism.
3. Review these objectives and progress towards them regularly throughout the programme. Be prepared to discuss them with facilitators and fellow delegates. Seek feedback.
4. Try to suspend disbelief. Do not be overcritical of exercise reality or relevance, but look for allegories and similarities with work and life.
5. Enjoy it.
6. Challenge and experiment. Examine theory with a critical eye, valuing it in your own terms, but be prepared to try new ideas and behaviours.
7. Consider the learning needs of other delegates. Understand how some have complementary and some contradictory objectives, help them to progress and give honest, constructive feedback.
8. Before leaving the programme, set new objectives and write an action plan.
9. Offer feedback to course designers and facilitators on appropriateness and effectiveness of the programme.
10. On return to work, review learning objectives with others, share and invite comment on the action plan, revising it as necessary and then DO IT!

Figure 5.1 *How to get the most from an MDO programme as a delegate.*

One of the best ways of helping the transferability of learning is for delegates to have some time with their manager and the trainer, covering such areas as:

- Course objectives and how well they were met.
- How best to retain and reinforce learning.
- Actions initially arising out of the programme, how they are to be monitored, and what help is required.
- Further learning objectives that may have arisen.
- Feedback on the course and its effectiveness.

It might also be appropriate for all delegates to meet together a few months after the programme, as this provides excellent opportunities to jog fading memories and reactivate flagging action plans.

DIY Options

Although 'hard' outdoor programmes require highly skilled outdoor technical and safety specialists, lightweight 'outdoor experiential' exercises need only common sense, clear safety rules, and a modicum of safety wear.

Much can be achieved by a trainer using limited and inexpensive resources. Venues such as the company car park or sports field usually suffice and equipment need not be specialized or expensive. An able resource investigator can make use of many items to be found on the premises.

Some simple exercises and their uses are listed at the end of the chapter. They can be modified to address different aims or to accommodate particular constraints. Once a trainer has become competent at operating these and adapting them to a variety of process needs, it is a short step to designing completely new exercises.

Designing and running exercises is an excellent way to gain real insights into the MDO process. We emphasize that design is not easy, as there are a wide variety of factors to consider, and even the wording of written exercise-briefs, for example, needs an almost legalistic brain if loopholes are to be avoided. Specialists are still necessary – depth of expertise takes years to acquire – but a little design knowledge helps purchasers to be more discerning in using the outdoors.

The key to success for the trainer in any of the suggested exercises is in the review process. Some guidelines are offered in Chapter 8.

Designing New Exercises

Once the basic techniques are mastered, there are no special secrets in designing experiential exercises, whether of the indoor or outdoor type. As in many areas of endeavour, necessity is the mother of invention and identifying a training need or dissatisfaction with known exercises is often the stimulus to designing better ones. A good exercise will pass the following tests:

- Does it highlight the right training need?
- Is it achievable by people of normal physique?
- Is it pitched at the right level of difficulty?

- Is there more than one solution?
- Are there enough resources?
- Is the time limit right?
- Is the exercise safe?
- Is the written brief clear of errors, omissions, ambiguities and loopholes?

If the answer to all the above questions is 'yes', then the next step is to stage a trial run, inviting feedback from colleagues. Incorporate any lessons into the final written brief.

Even when these tests have been applied, the exercise may not work as expected. Delegates have an unerring knack of finding new solutions, ambiguities in the brief, and ways of bypassing the constraints. These should not be viewed as setbacks, but rather as a natural part of the design and development process. Such unexpected alterations often lead to new ideas and exercises.

There are many exercises common to MDO organizations, and arguments as to origin and authorship are widespread. We claim no exclusive rights to the exercises that follow (although we *know* we designed some of them!), but are happy to share them with you.

Sample Exercises

Exercise 1: Up in the Air

Aims: Teamwork, problem solving, leadership.

Physical resources: Scaffold poles, scaffold spanners, string, planks, safety helmets.

Time: 20–30 minutes.

Brief: The task is to get the entire team two feet (0.6m) off the ground for at least 60 seconds.

Constraints: The structure must be self supporting. Only equipment provided may be used.

Variations: With increased resources, simple price list and a budget, resource planning can be considered.

Safety: Watch for carelessness in handling equipment, particularly long steel poles. Intervene on obviously unstable structures.

Exercise 2: Odd One Out

Aims: Teamwork, problem solving, leadership.

Physical resources: A marked area with two boundaries 14 feet apart.

At point A:
2 long scaffold poles; scaffold clips; 100ft (30m) rope; helmets; gloves.

At Point B:
3 long scaffold poles; 100ft (30m) rope; scaffold spanner; 5-gallon (25 litres) container of water.

Time: 20–30 minutes

Brief: The entire team is to cross from point A to point B, and take with it the 5-gallon container of water. One team member may be placed at point B before starting.

Constraints: No-one may go around the area; nothing may touch the ground between A and B; the container may not be thrown or touched directly; only equipment provided may be used.

Safety: Watch for carelessness in handling equipment, particularly long steel poles. Intervene on obviously unstable structures. Ensure caution if equipment is thrown. Supervise lifting of container, adjust size/weight as appropriate.

Exercise 3: Barrels and Planks

Aims: Teamwork, problem solving, leadership.

Physical resources: A marked area; three oil drums/barrels; two 6 ft (2m) planks.

Time: 20 minutes.

Brief: The task is to move the entire team from one side of the marked area to the other.

Constraints: No team member may touch the ground inside the marked area or walk around it. The planks may not touch the ground inside the marked area.

Penalties: If a plank or individual touches the ground the team must restart.

Safety: Beware of barrels rolling from under participants. Watch for trapped fingers between barrels and planks. Gloves reduce the chance of picking up splinters.

Exercise 4: Bucket Balance

Aims: Teamwork, problem solving, leadership

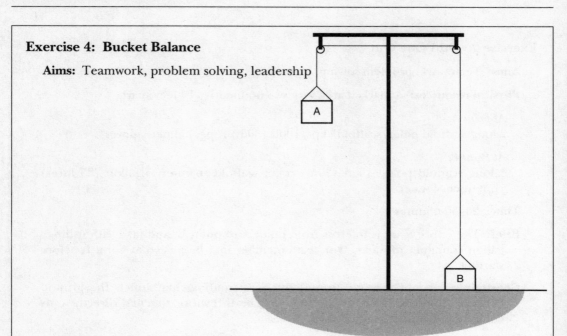

Physical resources: Two buckets arranged as per the diagram and connected through pulleys (the lower bucket contains about a pint (0.5 litres)of water); marked area of approx. 6ft (2m) square; sundry lengths of pipe and hose, max 6ft (2m) long; sticky tape; plastic mug; bucket of water.

Time: 20 minutes.

Brief: The task is to change the balance of the buckets so that bucket A touches the ground and bucket B is up in the air.

Constraints: No team member may touch the ground inside the marked area. No equipment may touch anything, including the ground inside the marked area. Only equipment provided may be used.

Safety: Watch for carelessness in handling equipment.

Geographical Exercises

Some examples of these are described in Chapter 7, but are mentioned here as they are simple to design for any area, including built up ones and are, therefore, a DIY option. Resources, such as maps, plans or *A to Z* books are easily obtainable.

ACTIVITY 5

We recall with a shudder the manager who seemed to want a perfectly routine outdoor development programme, but who on the journey to the training centre told the rest of his team that if they chose not to abseil, they were also choosing not to turn up for work the next week. You can imagine the state of some of the delegates.

Over the following days the issue slowly emerged. How could such an issue be made to help the group?

6 Choosing the Right Provider

▷   SUMMARY   ◁

In this chapter we deal with the actions required of the company training/HR specialist to ensure the full benefits of the outdoors are gained.

- We point out the importance and methods of clearly identifying learning objectives.
- We suggest ways of comparing providers of MDO and how to choose the one most appropriate to your needs
- We discuss the relative merits of open or company courses, and of standard or tailored programmes.

After reading the chapter you should be able to:

- Identify and clarify learning objectives, for both individuals and groups.
- Identify the essential criteria for your ideal provider.
- Recognize the different benefits of open and company, standard and tailored courses and choose the best one for your company.

Every manager is responsible for ensuring that expenditure is justifiable and cost effective.

A manager buying a new piece of machinery or office equipment would consider factors such as:

- Why it is wanted.
- Suitability of various models.
- Alternative suppliers.

- Demonstrations and trials.
- Capital and running costs.
- After sales service.
- Payback period.

When expenditure is by a training department the justification needs to be even stronger – it will also be appraised by the client department. External courses are expensive – usually more so than other training costs.

Fortunately, there are ways of checking credentials and identifying and confirming standards. Our aim in this chapter is to offer some thoughts on how to go about this, including questions to ask and areas to consider. A checklist similar to the one above but for purchasing courses is:

- Clearly identify learning objectives.
- Comparing courses – open or company, standard or tailored?
- Alternative suppliers.
- Sample/pilot courses.
- Design and delivery costs.
- Follow up.
- Evaluation.

We will consider all of these in this chapter.

Learning Objectives

The prior clarification of learning objectives is a very important aspect of any training programme and should never be neglected. It is, however, worth emphasizing its importance *prior to* MDO programmes because potential delegates often assume that outdoor programmes have unique aims and objectives, such as personal fulfilment and 'toughening up the troops'.

While people often do achieve personal fulfilment on MDO programmes, this varies from person to person and is rarely sufficient justification for significant expenditure. The maximum benefit from MDO programmes comes when there are clearly identified and communicated objectives. There are many reliable methods of establishing training needs and programme objectives, including:

- interviews, with staff and management;
- observation;
- questionnaire surveys;
- appraisal systems; and
- organizational analysis.

Any combination of these will assist the training specialist in effectively identifying training needs and course objectives.

The assistance of outside consultants is also an option, and many training organizations offer such a service, although there are dangers in involving them as sometimes they have a vested interest in recommending their own training programme! Most training managers will naturally prefer to conduct their own needs survey, acting as an internal consultant. (There are appropriate and useful titles in this Practical Trainer Series published by Kogan Page; a series list will be found at the front of this volume.)

Whatever methods are used, the more clearly the objectives are identified the better the chances of a successful programme. It is equally important to ensure that all delegates are fully briefed about the objectives, methods and nature of the course (see Chapter 5).

Sometimes company training staff are their own worst enemies. We remember a group of senior managers arriving on an outdoor programme, their company's training manager having provided only a knowing smile, the starting time, and the location. They came in business suits, not knowing what to expect and felt insecure and antagonistic. These feelings increased on discovering that they were about to embark on five days of outdoor activities. The first two days were spent allaying fears, building trust and establishing some credibility; time (and cost) wasted.

Course Types

Having decided what is to be achieved the company trainer needs to consider whether to send the delegates on an open course or a special company-focused course. There are advantages to each:

Open
- Can be used as a sampler to evaluate provider.
- Can accommodate small number of delegates with like needs.
- Gives opportunities for cross-fertilization with managers from other companies and industries.
- Has most of the advantages of a standard course as outlined below.

Company
- Options for customizing or tailoring.
- Allows influence over content and style.
- Opportunities for cross fertilization between departments, disciplines and sites.
- There is a possibility of direct involvement by company training staff.
- There is potential for bonding, and improving work relationships.

Discussions internally and with suppliers will help the training manager to make this crucial decision. A mixture of the two may also be an option, with some major training needs being met on a company-focused course and others, only applicable to a small number, on a suitable open course. It may be an advantage to send a delegate on an open course to evaluate the programme, possibly the training manager.

The bespoke course has some obvious advantages. It should be more specific, addressing exact training needs, and will better reflect the company's culture and values. To achieve those ideals it is necessary to use reputable and experienced suppliers and to have a thorough understanding of both the medium and the organization's needs.

The off-the-shelf option should certainly be cheaper and available at shorter notice. If the identified training needs are relatively simple and broad, this option may well be suitable. There is also the compromise option of customizing an open course. This can sometimes give the best of both worlds.

There are benefits and drawbacks to both the bespoke and the off-the-shelf approaches, so we will examine each in some detail.

Standard Courses

These have much to recommend them. The cost should be lower and the exercises tried, trusted, and well understood by the provider's staff. Outcomes tend to be satisfactorily predictable. Disadvantages include a mismatch between clients' needs and the programme content, and sometimes reduced energy levels in course staff.

Costs should be lower because the amount of pre-course work for the provider is greatly reduced. From our experience, it takes about half as much time to prepare a five-day repeat programme as to put together an all new event. This means that staff are more often available to work on other programmes and the provider can get through more courses in a year at minimal additional cost. As an illustration of this, one well-known and successful provider expects their staff to clock up around 200 course-days each year; bespoke providers tend to manage 100–140 days a year.

It should be noted that some providers quietly ignore the savings and many clients don't ask for reductions for repeat programmes. Would you expect to pay the same for your 50th ream of paper or 5000th washer as for your first? Indeed, one of the most expensive providers of all has been continually running a highly standardized programme for many years. Many purchasers don't even ask why provider A's standard package costs the same as supplier B's tailored programme. There may be good reasons for this, but it is as well to ask.

Familiarity

The use of tried and trusted exercises and programmes brings another advantage. It is much easier to forecast the outcome of an exercise once it has run for the Nth time. It is also makes the day-to-day logistics much simpler because every staff member knows almost without thinking where to be and what to do at any given time. They are also more likely to note and react to deviations, recognize problems and deal with them. So there is much less risk of a programme going off the rails. As in life, so in MDO, change brings risks.

Disadvantages

There are some risks in running standard packages. Course staff can become bored and start to miss important processes, lacking energy when delivering overfamiliar inputs and, at worst and only rarely, adopting a casual attitude towards safety.

A more insidious danger is that presented by the culture prevalent in some standard course providers. We have observed that centres operating in this way not unnaturally tend to attract staff who like the security of knowing everything inside out. Consequently, when there is an outbreak of non-standard learning – and it does happen even on the most standard of programmes – the staff are unable or unwilling to handle it. They have their learning lists and they are sticking to them! If delegates are attending the programme to enable them to cope better with change, or to challenge comfort zones, this can be very frustrating and counter productive.

An even greater risk is that the programme may not match the client's needs. It is nowadays clear that any organization, composed as it is of unique individuals, and possessing as it does a unique history, tends to have a distinct culture. This means it will have unique strengths, weaknesses and development needs. An off-the-shelf course needs to be very good indeed to meet the needs of every different culture.

Choosing a standard course

A number of large providers run regular open courses dealing with a variety of objectives. Some even specialize in it, to the exclusion of tailored courses. In some notable cases this approach has been very successful, and there are ample referees to its effectiveness.

Some providers have developed the art to the extent of running series of open courses, thus covering all aspects of management development, albeit with a very broad brush. There are courses for graduates and trainee managers, for supervisors and more senior personnel. When considering an off-the-shelf option, look for a 'best fit' against your own objectives. Seek feedback from people who know the course. If time and funds allow, send yourself or a reliable deputy on the course – better to spend a little money checking a programme than to waste credibility and cash on something that fails to meet your organization's needs.

Customized off-the-shelf programmes

It is unlikely that you will find an open course that is perfect for your needs. Like an off-the-peg suit it will require some adjustments to fit your measurements and style – your needs and culture.

We therefore recommend that you examine not only overall course objectives, but also individual exercise aims, constraints and expected solutions before accepting them as suitable. It is equally vital to consider the content and style of review sessions.

Having identified anomalies or undesirable elements you should be able, with the provider, to make the necessary adjustments. You will also better understand what your people are liable to get out of the course and may come up with ideas that are adopted by the supplier.

This approach can give you many of the benefits of a bespoke course at the pre-packaged price, but will require time and effort. It also precludes attendance as a delegate. If such is a requirement, all you can do is discuss your needs in detail and trust to the supplier for their fulfilment.

Conclusion

In our experience, standardized programmes are good for addressing the common developmental denominators but lack an edge when it comes to dealing with issues peculiar to one organization. They are a low-risk option. A few pounds might be saved, nothing will go wrong, but potential gains are limited. They are also a practical way of evaluating the medium and the provider!

Tailored Programmes

These too have advantages and drawbacks. The main advantage is that they stand a much better chance of addressing the client's real and unique needs. Further advantages are that the energy levels of course staff can be much higher, and this tends to be communicated to delegates, often with beneficial results.

The main disadvantage is the risk involved in breaking new ground. In addition, the financial cost can sometimes be high.

Addressing real needs

Despite the drawbacks of longer lead time and increased costs, only a tailored programme can hope to meet the particular needs of an organization. Providers who specialize in this kind of work can be highly skilled at researching and defining training needs, often using sophisticated tools. Many run workshops before the programme to ensure that they are getting the needs right.

All this costs time and money, but can lead to programmes which make a real contribution to change and improvement.

Fresh as tomorrow

Another advantage of tailored programmes is that by their very nature they always include fresh material which means that course staff have to be alert to what is happening within groups. This often has a mirroring effect on delegates, who seem to become much more process sensitive and energized. Similarly, organizations offering tailored programmes tend to attract people who like to live with variety and change.

From our observations, these people seem to be very alive to process issues, and happy to pursue things as they develop.

The risks of pioneering

All tailored programmes incur the risks involved in something new. There may be untried exercises. There may be misconceptions about the group's learning needs or even hidden agendas of development needs. Untried exercises tend to work well if the providers are skilled and experienced. Good providers acquire a feel for what will and won't work, for timescales, and for appropriate levels of physical exertion.

Misconceptions about group learning needs are more of a problem. The answer is never to buy anything before having checked the *why* as well as the *how* of each exercise with the provider. Hidden agendas such as the one in Activity 6 (p 88) are similarly difficult and it takes an astute provider to handle them. If you suspect they may exist, you should share this with the provider, and jointly decide how they are to be handled. It can be very dangerous to ignore such issues as they can distort or even negate any progress towards group development.

Safety

Despite habitually working with new material, there is nothing to choose between standard and bespoke providers in this area. In both cases high standards are generally the rule and in both cases there are regrettable exceptions.

Choosing or co-designing a bespoke course

For providers this is a successful, rewarding and sometimes profitable option. It allows them the time and opportunity to develop new material, which can also be used in future open courses.

For the buyer, it allows specific needs to be more directly addressed, company culture to be better reflected and gives greater control over the learning environment.

N.B. While becoming accustomed to using the cycle, there are two keys to sucess:
1. Do not move on to the next step until you have completed the one before.
2. Review against objectives.

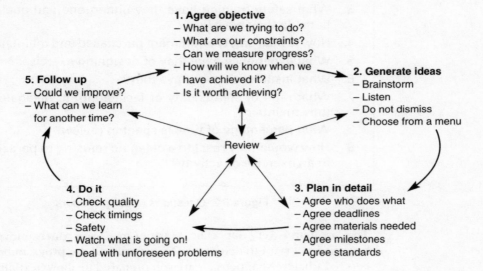

1. Agree objective
– What are we trying to do?
– What are our constraints?
– Can we measure progress?
– How will we know when we
  have achieved it?
– Is it worth achieving?

2. Generate ideas
– Brainstorm
– Listen
– Do not dismiss
– Choose from a menu

5. Follow up
– Could we improve?
– What can we learn
  for another time?

Review

4. Do it
– Check quality
– Check timings
– Safety
– Watch what is going on!
– Deal with unforeseen problems

3. Plan in detail
– Agree who does what
– Agree deadlines
– Agree materials needed
– Agree milestones
– Agree standards

Figure 6.1 *The problem-solving circle*

If there is a requirement for a series of courses with a large training population, the extra cost of design is easily justified. Often however, the requirement is for a one-off course to address a particular need. In this case the bespoke course is often the only effective option. When costing this option, be sure to take the hidden costs represented by your own time into account, and try to secure some kind of ceiling on supplier's preparation time. Many suppliers are happy to agree a fixed price for preparation.

Most of the suggestions made for customizing a course apply here even more strongly. Take the following into account:

- course objectives;
- exercise aims;
- constraints set by physical and safety factors;
- time allowed for review sessions;
- expected content of those sessions;
- flexibility of the programme.

1. What is their training philosophy?
2. What industrial or commercial experience do their staff have?
3. What safety training have they undergone and qualifications do they have?
4. How is their safety equipment purchased and maintained?
5. What experience have they of designing exercises?
6. What insurance cover have they?
7. What ratio of staff (safety or facilitating) to delegates do they maintain?
8. What percentage of time is spent in review?
9. How would they react to a delegate refusing to participate in an exercise or activity?

Figure 6.2 *Questions to ask providers*

The last item is very important as issues may arise which unexpectedly become important to delegates. Do you want all the programmed items covered whatever happens, or are you prepared to allow flexibility? If so, how much? In effect, the more deeply involved the client's training staff make themselves, the more bespoke and less off-the-shelf courses become.

Figure 6.1 describes in detail a method for working effectively with providers. It is adapted from a well-known model for project management, but we have found it to be highly effective.

Conclusion
Tailor-made programmes fit particular training and development needs much more snugly than standard products. They can be really valuable tools for helping to transform organizational cultures. They may cost more initially, but they represent a 'high gain' option, with all that entails.

You must, however, ensure that providers can deliver what they say they can. In the larger development training organizations design and delivery are sometimes separated. What is well understood by the designers may be misunderstood or misinterpreted by the deliverers.

Choosing a Supplier

A bewildering array of organizations provide or claim to provide MDO. These vary from large organizations through to small specialist providers. Some exclusively supply MDO, others offer a broader range of programmes. Some useful questions to ask are suggested in Figure 6.2. Whatever the type of organization, standards and capabilities vary enormously.

As well as a clear idea of what is wanted from a supplier, areas to consider include:

- **Cultural compatibility** Some organizations have very clear cultures and philosophies. This can be a great benefit if they are compatible with the client company. If compatibility is incomplete, problems can arise. We know of a provider who strongly advocated Transactional Analysis. This is a very powerful training tool, but there are others. They provided it to the exclusion of all else. Delegates muttered of 'Analysis Paralysis', and clients moved on. The organization almost folded before its senior employees saw sense.

- **Experience of staff** Although outdoor skills are important and safety paramount, it is usually as important for training staff to have at least some experience of the business world. An HR director once talked to us of his frustration with his previous supplier, staffed as he put it by 'well intentioned abseilers'.

- **Location** It may be entirely appropriate and desirable for delegates to travel long distances to wilderness regions, but time, cost and the inconvenience of travelling should be taken into account. Some providers are tied to one particular geographical area, others more mobile, some totally peripatetic.

- **Accommodation provided** Some providers have their own accommodation, ranging from very well equipped country houses to mountain huts. Others operate from hotels of varying standards, sometimes with mutually supportive agreements. Still other providers expect delegates to live in tents or makeshift bivouacs. The appropriate choice depends on the objectives of the programme and the costs.

- **Levels of physicality** Programme objectives, physical fitness, and the expectations of the delegates all have a bearing on the level of physicality of a course. The options in this area are covered in some detail in Chapter 3.

Finding, Visiting and Evaluating Suppliers

Suppliers of MDO can be found through the usual channels – exhibitions, conferences, advertisements and so on. In addition, word-of-mouth recommendation is a popular way of finding good suppliers. Whatever the reputation of a supplier, we would strongly advise that they be visited, preferably when a course is in residence.

Even then, there are a number of potential pitfalls for the unwary. Beware of organizations that:

- design and run very physical programmes, claiming that this tests delegates' fitness to lead, unless this is clearly what is required;
- attempt to pressure delegates into inappropriate activities, such as the organization which asks delegates what they would least like to do and then makes them do it. Is this ever appropriate to legitimate learning objectives?
- demand that delegates take part in domestic duties, such as cleaning or cooking, describing it as part of the experience, when in fact it is to reduce staff costs. There *are* occasions when such chores can provide valuable learning, but not often and only when properly reviewed;
- claim to tailor programmes, but in fact always run the same programme;
- programme long periods of outdoor activities – pure climbing, caving and the like – as opposed to exercises with clear learning objectives;
- profess to spend time in review, but in fact only ask if the activity was enjoyed or conduct a very short, informal session.

Other Points to Consider

Sample and Pilot Courses

A number of organizations offer sampler weekends and similar short programmes, which can provide a useful and inexpensive way of evaluating the supplier but are often of short duration, and therefore of dubious value. A more reliable method is to attend an open course, where things can truly be viewed from the delegate's angle.

For those needing to send large numbers of delegates, the option of a pilot course makes great sense, giving both the client and the supplier the opportunity to fine-tune the programme.

Design and Delivery Costs

To measure value and compare prices it is helpful to separate the costs of course design and delivery. Effective course design may require (and the cost therefore include):

- company visits and familiarization tours;
- training needs analysis;
- interviews with delegates;
- psychometric questionnaires;
- pre-course briefings.

The duration, scope and cost of these should be discussed and agreed beforehand. Although design days usually cost less than delivery days, they may comprise a significant proportion of the total price. While a company training officer, one of the authors neglected this and received a bill 15 per cent higher than expected. Follow up time, if appropriate, should be similarly timed and costed.

The cost of delivery days is usually fully inclusive, but beware of extras, such as equipment hire, transport costs, etc. Accommodation is usually a large part of the cost. If dedicated accommodation is not used, consider who should book and cost it. Some suppliers have valuable mutual arrangements, but some organizations have more buying power.

Follow Up

This oft neglected area can be crucial to the lasting success of any training programme. This is especially so for an MDO programme, where the transfer of learning back to the 'real world' is vital for success.

The need for follow up and its format should be decided beforehand, along with the number of design days and course duration. The need, content, duration and cost should all be discussed. It will not always be appropriate or necessary for the provider to be involved.

Action planning – 'How I intend to apply the learning back at work' – is a common and important part of any training programme. It is also the most frequently and quickly forgotten part! Follow up can reinforce and facilitate this process, particularly if delegates' managers and training staff are involved.

Evaluation

Evaluation of the training will help to decide whether objectives have been achieved and also whether the medium and the supplier should be used again. It should be as carefully planned and executed as the course itself and done at the same time.

Evidence to support the effectiveness of MDO programmes is scarce and largely apocryphal. Reliance on course review forms, or 'happy sheets', ticked after a fun weekend in the hills, is unscientific and often misleading.

Training evaluation should be a continual process, with delegates and their managers asked several times for their feedback. Only then can it be established whether the training met its stated objectives and if there is any relationship with achievement of company goals.

ACTIVITY 6

A group is given a two-hour orienteering task in steep (but precipice-free) woodland terrain. The going underfoot could be described as appalling. The redeeming feature of the area is that it is crossed by well-made tracks which weave gently up the sides of the steep hills, providing a longer but shallower and easier means of navigation.

The leader of the group, having read the brief, reveals that in a previous life he flew fighter planes, and therefore has a good grasp of navigation and an airman's compass. He overrules the polite objections of his colleagues, pockets all the maps, squints at the compass, and marches off into the wild, closely followed by the rest of the group. Four hours later, covered in mud, bracken and perspiration, they emerge.

What are the likely outcomes of review? More importantly, what might the leader and the group learn from the task?

---

7 Outdoor Media and Methodology

▷   SUMMARY   ◁

In this chapter we explore the media and methodology of MDO, including:

- Outdoor media, and how they are used:
  - lightweight exercises;
  - navigation-based media;
  - rockface options;
  - water-based activities;
  - underground tasks.
- Ways in which these media are combined to form exercises applicable to management development.

After reading this chapter, you will:

- Have a user's (but not a professional's) working knowledge of the most frequently-used outdoor media.
- Be able to make effective judgements about the applicability of particular outdoor exercises to MDO.

In this chapter, we examine the main vehicles for outdoor training as applied to managers. Each section will deal with a particular medium, and will include examples or cases to consider. We will also examine ways in which the various media may be combined.

Although tasks and simulations are very important, we strongly emphasize that exercises are merely the means by which MDO produces raw experiential data. That data ought to be processed to be understood, so review – which we examine in the next chapter – ought to be seen as at least of equal importance.

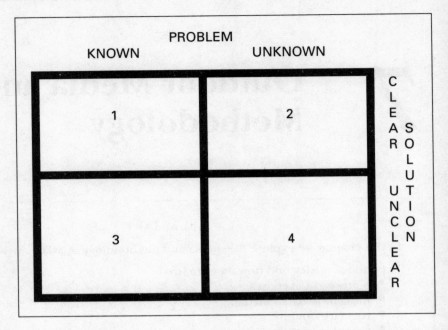

Figure 7.1 *Problem definition window* (derived from the work of Roy Williams and Chris Creswick)

This is a lesson which some MDO practitioners do not understand. Others lack the life-experience to review properly. Any trainer seeking to place an MDO programme should recognize that *process skills are as important as exercise design and running skills* and purchase accordingly.

There are a variety of outdoor media – microlight flying and sub-aqua work, for example – which we have omitted from this section either because they have only limited application to MDO or because they are so highly specialized. Nevertheless, in the six sections that follow, we believe we not only cover the territory of the vast majority of outdoor exercises, but also give powerful hints as to how to use other media.

As this is a book about MDO, we make only passing reference to other perfectly valid experiential media such as the use of drama. This does not imply any criticism. As part of the process of examining outdoor exercises, we often use the Williams–Creswick Window, as shown in Figure 7.1, a useful tool for determining the level of complexity of a problem, whether it is an outdoor exercise or a work-related matter.

Lightweight Exercises

The WOSB exercise (see Chapter 1) has a host of descendants in the form of a very wide and growing variety of tasks lasting anything from five minutes to five hours or more. In terms of the Williams–Creswick window, they fit in anywhere from boxes 1 to 3, and, in combination, box 4 (see Figures 7.2–7.4).

Some of the exercises have been around for a very long time indeed, and it is a perpetual source of surprise to us that succeeding generations of managers continue to be confounded by them.

Definition

The term 'lightweight exercises' can be misleading because some tasks, if carried out without planning, can be anything but light. We therefore clarify our definition to encompass *those tasks which can be carried out on the equivalent of a football field* and which require *little or no preparation apart from providing the brief, equipment and safety input.*

Uses

Lightweight exercises have a variety of uses including:

Icebreakers There are a number of very light exercises involving minimal equipment which are extremely useful for breaking down barriers of reserve between delegates. Often these exercises (like all good outdoor exercises) have useful spinoffs in that they may also address other process issues, depending on what issues happen to be 'live' with the group at the time. In one of our favourites, a group is taken to a car park or soccer field, blindfolded, given a 100ft (30m) rope, and asked to form a square resembling a boxing ring. This seemingly simple task has led to very many extremely useful reviews.

Building trust/bonds between delegates There are a variety of exercises which, although not intrinsically dangerous, certainly *feel* so when being carried out. These tasks are useful because they stimulate mutual trust and a recognition of the need for appropriate encouragement. In some cultures this is a valuable lesson indeed.

A danger is that they may turn into 'initiation ceremonies' with those who fail to complete the task feeling excluded. This is a serious issue, and one which we discuss in detail at the end of this chapter. Nonetheless, 'trust exercises' can teach very valuable lessons.

The Trust Task

A group (numbering eight or so) is asked to remove all sharp or hard items such as watches or identity chains from their wrists and then is taken to a field on which a stepladder has been firmly placed. The highest step is around two metres from the ground. Group members are invited to face each other in two equal rows about 2ft (60 cm) apart with hands held out palms upward, as if carrying a large tray, with the steps of the ladder at one end of the avenue thus formed.

The trainer should ensure that the delegates' forearms form a fairly solid and level 'bed' on which to fall, and then should explain that s/he is going to climb the ladder and fall backwards into the waiting arms of the group. This s/he does, after checking the group's readiness, falling backwards with body held stiff and hands clasped loosely in front of them. The group have no difficulty holding the trainer because even 240lb, shared between eight people, only works out at 30lb (14kg) each. This will, of course, be distributed unevenly, but even so, the most anyone would hold should be 50lb or so.

Thereafter, the trainer invites the group to do the same, one after the other. A further rule is that delegates may individually choose the step from which they are to fall.

The positive feelings liberated by this exercise can be very strong indeed.

Figure 7.2 *Example of a box 1 exercise*

Problem-solving Many lightweight box 2 and 3 exercises actually are problems waiting to be solved. We have therefore found them to be ideal in giving people practice in using disciplined problem-solving techniques in real situations with real pressures, real time-constraints and real targets.

The format for the session is to break the ice with something physically light and with some problem-solving 'meat' in it. Review then focuses on the latter, with the group identifying whatever appropriate issues arose from the task.

An input on the problem-solving cycle (see Figure 6.1) would follow, and then groups would be invited to use it in the task that followed. Subsequent review would include a focus on the cycle, as well as any other issues which might arise.

An area of ground 14ft (4.3m) wide is roped-off with pegged string at ground level to form a 'no-go' area. Equipment is placed on each side as follows:

Side A: Three 12ft. (3.5m) scaffold poles; one 100ft (30m) 8mm polypropylene rope; a large supply of scaffold clips; one 5-gallon (25 litre) container of water.

Side B: Two 12ft (3.5m) scaffold poles; one 100ft (30m) 8mm polypropylene rope; a spanner/wrench suitable for use with scaffolding.

The group's task is to transport itself and the water from point A to point B without either the equipment or any members touching the ground between the 14ft gap. The group may place one member at side B, but once that person is there, s/he must stay on that side.

The beauty of the task, for which we allow around 40 minutes, is that it has several solutions, some involving low physicality and high ingenuity, others the reverse. It lends itself perfectly to a properly disciplined problem-solving process.

In all cases, adequate safety precautions should apply, and appropriate clothing should be worn, including working gloves and site-helmets. Scaffolding is heavy and may have sharp edges.

Figure 7.3 *Example of a box 2 exercise*

Communication Working tasks are usually performed badly if instructions are unclear or deficient. Well-laid plans are useless unless clearly passed on. People often fail to reach their full potential if they feel that they are undervalued or ignored.

Communications – good, bad, or non-existent – are a major contributor to the success or failure of an enterprise. Therefore it should also figure in exercises; if people are able to make their communication mistakes in the relative safety of a course, they may save themselves real problems – incurring real costs – at work.

All exercises, of course, allow for the frailty of human communication simply by being tasks in which people have to interact. Particular aspects of communication can also be built into exercises.

An example is the exercise mentioned in the 'icebreakers' paragraph, in which delegates are blindfolded and thus deprived of the ability to interpret words in the context of their accompanying body language. This often helps them to reach the conclusion that they need to learn how to listen – a skill they can then practise for the duration of the programme. We will mention other examples in subsequent sections of this chapter.

Safety Because they lack the obvious hazards of cliff and cave, it is easy to ignore safety issues on lightweight exercises. This is unfortunate because some of them possess some potential for danger. We have found that two approaches lead to safety:

The worst-case scenario Put simply, we imagine the worst possible outcomes of an exercise, and then guard against them. This has led us to, for example, insist upon gloves and climbing helmets in scaffold exercises.

The coroner's court test Quite simply, could one stand up in a coroner's court and say that one had done all one could to protect a delegate? If the answer is not an unequivocal 'yes!', then one has problems.

Limitations of Lightweight Exercises

Using *only* short tasks can encourage a restricted repertoire of similar behaviours. Even if those behaviours are relevant to the job, delegates may experience some difficulty in making the mental transfer of the learning to the world of work when the exercises are seen as simplistic and repetitive.

If trainees see the exercises as an over-simplified simulation of the working environment, they may reject the experience as irrelevant.

Summary

Short-term 'grounds' exercises are useful because they:

- can be set up quickly and conveniently;
- do not require mountainous terrain;
- can be used in quick succession to build reviewable experience quickly;
- can be designed to focus on particular organizational/process issues.

They have limitations though, particularly if a whole day is spent on a series of similar exercises. Boredom with the limitations of, for example, scaffolding can set in very quickly.

We emphasize that the examples of themes that emerge from particular exercises are only some ways of using those exercises. There are dozens of other exercises, which can be used in hundreds of ways. The key is to be aware of the managerial and interpersonal processes.

Geographical Options

Outdoor education has traditionally used navigation-based exercises – everything from simple orienteering in local woodlands to wild country expeditions lasting several days – to build confidence, improve thinking under pressure, and enhance the physique.

Organizations at the more developmental end of the MDO spectrum have adopted and improved upon outdoor education exercises so that as well as (or instead of) achieving the above ends, they can be put to further use to generate progress in a variety of managerially related issues including:

- communication;
- planning;
- teamwork;
- decision-making;
- leadership;
- managing people;
- time management; and
- resource management.

Although there is an infinite variety of sub-classifications of geographical/ navigational exercises, there are two clear sub-genres:

Clue-searches on foot Ranging from simple orienteering for points through to exercises with complex payoff charts and deep behavioural undercurrents (see Activity 8 on p 121). As well as processes related to the above list, the physicality of on-foot exercise often adds interesting and useful ingredients in terms of the way that delegates treat each other. This can range from extreme mutual concern and support through to quite arrogant pressuring (see Activities 6 and 7 for examples, both of which are genuine).

Other geographical exercises There are a variety of developments of foot-based options, ranging from adding bicycles through to providing motor vehicles. In the latter case it is advisable to provide drivers, as a course member in pursuit of a deadline is not a particularly safe individual.

These exercises often have a wider application than standard orienteering tasks. Lots of additional elements can be incorporated, including:

- co-operation versus competition;
- managing remote teams;
- the need for an effective communication network.

We have often found that a time/performance element in the brief is very useful in enabling intelligent managerial analysis to be necessary to the task (see Activity 8 on p 121).

A mixed-media approach (feet, bicycles and cars) is also particularly useful if delegates are of a variety of levels of fitness. Although MDO is usually very safe, those accidents that have happened have tended to take place when people were pushed (or pushed themselves) too hard on navigational exercises. The presence of a vehicle allows people lacking in physical fitness to take a full part in tasks, as does the need for a central co-ordinating role.

Ropes and Rocks

Since the nineteenth century, rock climbing and mountaineering have been the consuming passions of a small section of society. Climbing has also been quite heavily used in outdoor education. Cliffs and crags have merit as development training media, although usually by being used in ways quite distinct from traditional rock sport. Unlike the media already examined, certain conditions must exist before rockwork can form part of a programme:

Special equipment It is not in the scope of this book to give an exhaustive list, but a few questions to providers are a useful way of establishing credibility. Examples are:

- The age and replacement-life of ropes used.
- How frequently the equipment is checked.
- Purchasing criteria.

Training Staff Although nationally known providers and those who have been in business for some years are generally very good, an organization's name is by no means a guarantee of the quality of its staff, and it is always worth asking a few difficult questions:

- The age and experience of staff.
- Their skill and qualifications.
- Qualification to supervise others.
- Ratio of trainees to instructors on rockface activities.

Model answers to the above questions, as related to rock climbing, spelaeology, sailing and canoeing are included in Appendix 1

Location Clearly, the distribution of rock faces limits the areas where climbing-related activities can take place. Even some apparently suitable venues do not meet the stringent safety standards required when working with people unfamiliar with rock faces.

One rock face we inspected and rejected was fine for free-climbing. Once ropes suitable for a novice group were rigged, however, a stream of small and not-so-small stones began falling from the top. There would have been a real risk of injury had we used the site with a group.

Rock face availability is further restricted by the unsuitability of most urban climbing walls, although we have found the occasional gem.

Development Training Limitations

Rock climbing is used by survival trainers as a means to apply pressure to delegates and by outdoor educators as a way of achieving peak experiences. Undiluted rock climbing, however, has only limited applications to true MDO for the following reasons:

- It is not a particularly corporate activity. The role of the group is largely limited to encouragement. The essence of rock climbing is a contest in which the individual climber pits herself or himself against a particular climbing route.
- It demands little of the group by way of organizational ability. Unless the group is very familiar with the equipment and with climbing practices in general, for them, climbing is reduced to just a rather frightening physical task that must be done.
- It can cause psychological damage – if everyone else has climbed and a bonus depends on you, you'll at least try. The fact that this is completely against your wishes may be ignored by the others.

Haul of Fame
The exercise lasts 150 minutes.

Earlier in the programme some of the group (six out of twelve or so) will have received training on the theory and practice of abseiling and upward hauling. The group's task, in two teams of six (the trained people spread equally among them), is to produce as large a profit as possible from units, each comprising one abseil and haul.

They will be paid 60p for each completed 'unit' to a maximum of 8 units. A bonus of £1.20 is payable if each member completes either one abseil, one haul, or manages the safety rope for ten minutes or more.

As always, the word of safety staff may not be challenged. As an added incentive to safety, each team will be fined 1 unit (i.e. 60p) for each infringement of safety rules, which are specified separately. **Safety staff observe at all times and delegates may not proceed over the edge or up the cliff without being checked by them**.

Delegates may purchase additional tuition on ropework from safety staff at a rate negotiable around one unit per five minutes.

At the end of the time allowed, the scores of each team are multiplied together, and the ensuing figure paid by staff to a charity of the group's choice. Should they sustain a loss, they will pay a charity of the staff's choice.

Figure 7.4 *Example of a box 2 or 3 exercise*

Undue pressure might be applied. Domination games might be played. It can even be perceived as an initiation, as in 'If you don't reach the top, you're not one of us!' The potential for psychological damage on a number of levels is clear.

Fortunately, there are a number of ways in which rock faces can be used to good effect. Many of these involve abseiling (rappelling in the USA) or mountain-rescue systems. Our particular preferences are:

- In multi-menu business games with climbing as one activity available from many, thus giving those who want to do it the opportunity, and those who wish to avoid it a chance to be useful elsewhere.

- As part of a mountain-rescue exercise, usually on a steep slope rather than on a cliff face. In this form, it can be combined with river crossing and navigation.
- As an abseiling/hauling business game in its own right, providing there are sufficient jobs for non-climbers to do.

Exercise 'Haul of Fame' (Figure 7.4) contains a number of points that make it eminently worth analysing as an example of how an MDO exercise differs from one intended for pure outdoor pursuits:

- Teams are free to compete or co-operate. Although the brief implies that co-operation gives the best financial result, this is often ignored. Potential for learning about working to a clear and correct strategy is obvious, as is the simple lesson that written information sometimes needs to be carefully read, rather than skimmed through.
- There is great learning potential around attitudes taken towards other work groups.
- There are many possibilities for learning how to encourage and support people appropriately in difficult situations.
- Learning for individuals might take a number of routes, ranging from facing up to fears through to learning about how to use positive feedback appropriately.
- The task is voluntary, but there is useful work to do – for example in hauling – for those who have no wish to abseil or be hauled. Thus the potential for humiliation is reduced.
- The exercise can very clearly be related to action-centred leadership (see Chapter 1) in that the leader must balance people's varying needs (some having a strong urge to 'have a go', others wanting very much not to, yet others open to persuasion) with the demands of the task (which actually can be most efficiently accomplished by sending one person up and down like a human yoyo) with team needs, perhaps around ensuring that the team does not split into two camps – for example, the doers and the haulers.
- All this is compounded by the mechanics of the task – quite complex – and political issues such as treatment of the other team. We have seen a wide spectrum of behaviours, ranging from portraying the other group as 'the opposition' through to complete and successful mergers.

In summary, cliffs and rock faces provide a useful medium of MDO provided:

- Exercises are designed to be relevant to managers' development needs.

- There is sufficient necessary and useful work for all levels of physicality and phobia.

Pure rock climbing is unlikely to meet these criteria, although the right group may well experience enjoyment and bonding.

Water-based Activities

The wide variety of water-based activities available even to those with access only to inland waters form a very popular development training, survival, and outdoor education medium. If a sea coast is at hand, the scope is even greater.

Given the wide choice of water-based activities, we will devote most of this section to an option-by-option look at the various options, covering:

- rafting;
- canoes and kayaks;
- light sailing vessels;
- large sailing vessels; and
- minor water-based activities.

Matters of general safety are incorporated into the text, as rules and good practice for each discipline are quite different. Appendix 1 contains details of the recommended qualifications for trainers to oversee the activities.

Rafting

Once again, a wide range of activities is covered by one word. It can mean anything from a skilled white-water activity to building something capable of supporting one delegate for a few minutes.

While all these have their applications, rafting is at its best as an MDO tool if the focus of exercises is on designing and building, as well as propelling, rafts. White water is dangerous territory in which to work and is best avoided. Even on still water, safety precautions should include appropriate buoyancy aids and independent safety boat.

Although this reduces the range to rafts which groups can realistically build, some of these vessels are quite impressive. We recall with great affection one vessel which dwarfed our safety boat and easily carried its international crew several miles across a Polish lake.

As well as simple design-and-build briefs, rafting exercises can address more sophisticated needs. They can be incorporated into business games by adding a cost/performance element, or can be tools in larger exercises. We set out an example in Figure 7.5

We once ran an exercise which involved over 80 delegates. Their task was to divert a stream across a lake. The only way to do this was to build a floating pipeline. Although rafts were not the central focus of the task, they were invaluable as construction vessels, and there were many agonized meetings with clients about raft costs, construction time, delivery promises, and best designs.

So protracted were these meetings that the workforce (in working life the peers of the 'Management') became disaffected and threatened strike action.

Management found itself caught between the rock of its customers and the hard place of a discontented workforce. This was an accurate reflection of their working environment, except that they could now see (and feel) *why* the work-force at the factory was discontented and *why* their real customers were finding other sources of supply. This gave them the resolve to deal with the real problems that their business faced.

They worked on their problems during the simulation to the extent that they actually achieved success in the task. They also took some very valuable learning home with them, and began to make efforts to improve human relations at work.

Figure 7.5 *Rafting exercise as part of something larger*

Kayaks and Canoes

Kayaks are descendants of the ancient Eskimo means of transport, effectively watertight because the boat is completely covered except for a close-fitting cockpit from which the occupant's body protrudes. Most kayaks are for one person, sometimes two.

Canoes are open-topped, often resembling the conveyance favoured in the movies by native Americans and Canadian voyageurs. Nowadays these vessels are made from duralumin or, like many kayaks, from high-impact plastic. Most are designed to carry between two and four people.

Both types of boat are firm favourites in outdoor education. Kayaks also have a very keen hobbyist following, while open-topped canoes have found a niche around the world as fun boats and fishermens' friends, even being given small outboard motors.

Both have their uses in MDO, although this usefulness is limited in the case of kayaks by the fact that the vast majority are one-person vessels, making the scope for teamwork very narrow. Nevertheless, exercises can be devised which have development applications.

Anyone planning to run an MDO session using kayaks will first need to ensure that:

1. Instructors possess the relevant safety qualifications.
2. All delegates are properly instructed in the use of safety and buoyancy gear.
3. All delegates are happy to work on water and, as well as understanding safety procedures, are correctly wearing the right safety gear.
4. All delegates pass the relevant safety tests, including roll-and-escape drill.

There are a variety of other safety precautions, including the need for safety-boats and appropriate aids to buoyancy before a group can enter the water.

Canoes, often being multi-person vessels which are more stable than kayaks, are more suitable for MDO. Novices feel less threatened kneeling in an open boat than when sitting enclosed in a watertight cockpit. We have found that incorporating canoes into rafting or lakeside orienteering exercises can be useful. As with all MDO, the key is to ensure that the exercises have management as well as outdoor pursuits credibility.

Safety precautions for canoes on the water are much the same as for kayaks, with the exception of the escape drills.

Light Sailing Vessels

Sailing such craft as dinghies and cutters on lakes and coastal waters has been a feature of outdoor education since the earliest days of Outward Bound.

Small boats can be very useful in MDO because the disciplines of sailing require people to act as a team; to give and receive trust; to communicate clearly; to act quickly.

It therefore follows that the larger the crew, the more appropriate to MDO the vessel is likely to be. Just working a 30-foot cutter in a lively sea is a teambuilding experience in itself. Small dinghies are fine, but exercises have to be contrived if the teambuilding involves more than the two or three people needed to crew them.

One of the drawbacks of light sailing vessels is that weather and wind conditions can vary considerably from day to day, and even hour to hour. This can mean that a task which was well within the capacity of the group when it was planned becomes practically impossible for inexperienced sailors the next day. Designers of MDO programmes which involve light sailing vessels should thus be able to demonstrate flexibility of approach, in order to ensure that variable weather does not hamper group progress.

Safety for small boat sailing requires the usual qualifications, buoyancy aids and independently-powered safety boats.

Large Sailing Vessels

An attractive means of MDO is provided by the use of large sailing vessels which are professionally skippered. These craft – ketches, schooners, former coastal cargo vessels, sailing barges and others – offer vast and largely unexplored scope for management development. From the right source, they are surprisingly inexpensive to hire, and can add an international dimension to a programme.

The sailing world has been one of the slowest to recognize the need for developmental skills to augment the necessary 'hard' skills. When questioned, many sail trainers enthusiastically endorse the development potential of their medium, but hold to the belief that the experience itself is enough. It is not, and those considering using this medium would be wise to check the groupwork skills of the trainers, and consider bringing in specialist group workers if necessary.

Nevertheless, the claims of sail trainers are true:

- Larger vessels offer a 'whole' experience. People live with the consequences of their actions, 24 hours a day. This can even extend to such domestic matters as catering and routine maintenance, which is often in the charge of delegates.
- The complete nature of the experience makes it an almost perfect means of bonding teams.
- Tasks are undoubtedly real, with the progress of the vessel depending completely on the ability to work together of its crew – the delegates.

The generally high degree of professionalism of large sailing vessel masters and crews ensures that general safety standards are high.

Going Underground

Superficially, the worlds of spelaeology (caving) and sailing are complete opposites. Closer examination exposes some surprising similarities, principal among which is the fact that both offer a very wide range of experiences, from safe tasks for novices right through to high-risk, high-profile projects suitable only for experts.

We are solely concerned with applications within management development, but even so, underground media can be safely harnessed in a variety of ways. We will examine these in some detail in a later section.

Safety Matters

There are ways in which the underground can be very physically and psychologically dangerous, in the latter case perhaps needing even more care than other media.

As well as the basic safety precautions provided by good equipment and technical instructors, we suggest the following:

- Exercises should involve a combination of surface and underground work. Many people have a very real fear of the subterranean world, and it helps no-one to have such fears tested.
- Caves and mines should be used as a means to an end and not just for the experience itself.
- When underground, groups should move at speeds which are comfortable to the slowest members. Often the fittest (or, worst of all, the instructors) set the pace. At the least this is irritating for older and heavier people.

Pure spelaeology shares some of the shortcomings of rock climbing in that it is a highly technical and specialized pastime with its own skills, jargon and equipment. Cave exploration is even more limited than climbing to particular geographical areas, especially as some of those areas suffer from high concentrations of potentially harmful radon gas and underground activity ought to be avoided. The addition of mine exploring adds some non-caving territory to the list.

While there is always some place for survival training underground, management development needs, particularly those of teambuilding, project management and co-ordination can be well-served by the underground. We set out some cases below:

- *In multi-menu business games*: Used in much the same way as climbing and abseiling.
- *Rescue exercises*: The logistics of cave-rescue are often very complex, and can form the framework for excellent co-ordination and planning tasks, especially if a 'surface' element can be included, for example by building in the need to set up and operate support facilities at the cave mouth.
- *Survey exercises*: Spelaeologists produce highly accurate surveys of caves. Given simple equipment – compasses, tape-measures and

self-built clinometers – delegates can also exhibit surprisingly accurate work. If combined with a surface survey, the result is a really effective and absorbing teamwork exercise. An element of presentation skills can be added by building in a post-survey presentation on the group's findings.

- *Feasibility Studies*: Particularly useful in areas where safe abandoned mines can be accessed, such studies can make excellent box 3/4 exercises. They are especially appropriate because there is much for surface teams to do.

  Typically such studies might involve examining the underground and surface environment of an abandoned metal mine in order to make recommendations for future uses of the site. By adding costings into the brief, and giving a deadline time at which a presentation is to be made to an invited audience of local notables, real pressure can be built into the task.

Such exercises can last anything from several hours upwards. The longest one we know took one week, was a project-management programme, and involved producing an hour-long video which became the only significant visual record of a particular slate mine.* The benefits to the delegates included:

- *Project management*: The logistics of writing, directing and editing such a video to near-professional standards are complex.
- *Resource investigation*: delegates had to research local libraries and museums, find the surviving quarrymen, visit and interview them. In addition, they had to research historical matters beyond living memory from whatever published sources they could find.
- *Human relations skills*: The mine was situated in a proudly nationalistic part of Wales, and the group needed to convince locals of the worthiness of their intentions before gaining their full co-operation.

There were a variety of other learning points, but the project stands as an excellent example of what can be done with underground resources, given sufficient imagination.

The underground has much to recommend it but should never be a compulsory feature of programmes.

*The task was jointly developed by Bob Quinney of the Co-operative Management Centre and Richard Bartrop of Guideford Training, and was based at the Bryn Eglwys mine near Towyn in North Wales. It was a timely project – a few years later the underground parts of the mine became unsafe to visit, while the surface was obliterated by tree-planting.

Combination Exercises

Management learning can be facilitated particularly well by combining outdoor media. This can be in a variety of ways:

Outdoor Business Games

Typically made up of a vast variety of tasks, each with some 'cash' value. They can include really deep outdoor activities – caving, climbing, for example – or lightweight outdoors – synchro-skipping, stretcher building, and construction tasks. The key is to have many more tasks than the group can perform in the time available.

Usually an element of cost is involved – tasks have to be bought from staff at a fixed percentage of possible earnings, rent and rates have to be paid, punitive interest charges made, and so on. Complication is added by, for example, including large mandatory tasks to be performed at fixed times or by making the tasks the means to generate income to complete some focal task. We have often used an exercise where the group has to build and drive a radio-controlled car or aeroplane, but has to buy the parts from income gained through outdoor tasks.

Projects

Sometimes a project-based approach to large exercises can be useful. An example is to give a group 24 hours in which to prepare a presentation to the local tourist board on how the area in which the course is based could be promoted as an outdoor leisure area, with examples of weekend and full-week outdoor holidays, costs, hotel provision, PR required to sell the area, and so on.

The advantage of such an approach is that all control – in fact as well as in theory – is passed to the group. *They* control quality and quantity. *Their performance* is what gets (or fails to get) results. *Their* energy drives the task.

Genuine Tasks

The project-based approach can be taken a stage further to include tasks which are genuine in their own right. The underground project cited earlier in this chapter is a good example. Tasks can be combined to include, for example, a 'raising cash for charity' option in a business game. This has worked very well in helping groups to wrestle with the task of identifying and clarifying objectives.

Working 'In the Dark'

Still popular are 'suspended disbelief' exercises, which stimulate the imagination as well as help managers to cope with ambiguity. In these exercises, groups are given a task and minimal information (to start with) to achieve it. Our own brand starts with the words 'John Doe is missing ... investigate'. The group are also given Doe's last known whereabouts and some background information.

From there on, things become more and more complicated with midnight rendezvous, shadowy networks, weird gnostic sects, industrial spies, coded messages, ecology-destroying substances and so on making an appearance.

If such tasks seem a little unreal, do not underestimate the imaginative powers of executives. People know that they are in an exercise, but nevertheless become really involved. The problem is not an easy one to solve - it requires *real* management skill and staff work to achieve the task. A further advantage is that most people are energized by involvement in such tasks.

This chapter clearly illustrates the point that there is more to the outdoors than is immediately obvious.

Whatever the medium, exercises should be focused on clear development needs. It is good for delegates to enjoy themselves, but it is not enough. Learning is only optimized by exercises which address real needs.

ACTIVITY 7

In exactly the same terrain as in Activity 6 (p 88), a group of retail section heads, led by their store manager, is given a complex orienteering-for-cash task, which they decide is best completed by splitting into four groups.

Penalties for lateness are punitive – the whole group's earnings are wiped out if three people are more than two minutes late. The start/finish point is at the end of a long, straight, track.

With five minutes to go, all but one team have returned. With three minutes to go, this team is spotted at the far end of the final straight. The whole team becomes voluble (but positive) in its encouragement. The latecomers start to run. Amid a barrage of applause they arrive one minute late, having thus reduced the group's profits by 50 per cent.

The manager's response is to console them, attempting to deflect the blame to herself for giving them too big a job. Their reaction is to seek to take the blame back on to their own shoulders.

What outcomes might be expected from review, and how might the task have affected the group's perception of its leader?

8   The Trainer as Facilitator

▷   SUMMARY   ◁

In this chapter we examine the work of group facilitation which underpins good MDO. In particular we will look at:
- The facilitator's role.
- Skills of facilitation and review.
- Some problems of review, and how to avoid them.

After working through this chapter, you should:
- Understand the role of the facilitator and the importance and limitations of its place in MDO and in review.
- Understand what skills are required for a facilitator to be effective.
- Understand ways in which groups avoid conflict, and how to handle this.

Facilitation – The Hidden Factor

Outdoor exercises are highly photogenic. The sight of managers doing interesting things on cliffs and moors has proved irresistible both to designers of brochures and directors of television documentaries.

An unfortunate consequence is that the very important area of review and group facilitation tends to be eclipsed. An understanding of the craft of facilitation is crucial for trainers working on MDO programmes. It is important for those who purchase them, as they will be more discerning in their decisions.

MDO programmes, even at the survivalist end of the spectrum, are not seriously aimed at teaching managers the skills of the outdoors, but at generating or highlighting the underlying human and mechanistic processes. Outdoor tasks merely exist to generate process in these two areas (see Figure 1.4). In effect, outdoor exercises are the means of generating data which are then considered in a number of ways during review, and include:

- personal reflection;
- small group discussions;
- small/large group reviews.

This is illustrated in Figure 8.1.

Task (data generation phase)
Outdoor, and designed so that the desired process issues will surface. For example, if a team is having problems because of submerged conflict between particular individuals, it is sensible to ensure that the task demands that they work together.

↓

Review (data processing phase)
During which individuals and groups are encouraged (see text for methods) to examine their behaviour and to reach conclusions about how to be more effective. Although it is often convenient for review to take place after tasks, this is by no means a cast iron rule. Review is often supplemented by inputs which can serve to 'legitimize' some discovery made by the group.

↓

Resolution (data modification phase)
A natural consequence of review is for individuals and groups to resolve to modify their behaviour. This phase can be followed by more tasks to test the viability of resolutions and to generate new data.

↓

Relating Back
If exercises have been properly designed or selected, and if review has been guided in the appropriate direction, learning will be applicable to people's work. Time should be spent planning exactly how to do this.

Figure 8.1 *The process of MDO*

Even without review it is probable that some learning takes place on outdoor programmes. Humans are not robots, and even the most task-centred programme provides some food for thought. Review, however, benefits programmes in the following ways:

- Learning can be shared and therefore multiplied.
- Learning can be focused towards helpful areas.
- Learning can be recorded before being forgotten.
- Additional interpersonal issues can be raised.
- Inappropriate lessons may be challenged.
- Reflection is guaranteed – not haphazard.

The Role of the Facilitator

Groups are helped – but merely helped – to learn by effective facilitators. Facilitators are what the name implies – not teachers or lecturers (although facilitating may occasionally require skills in this area) or people charged with getting a group through an exam, but people whose job is *to help others identify their own learning*. To smooth the path of discovery.

Group observation need not be the sole preserve of the trainer. It is a valuable skill which can be introduced to participants, who in turn may provide beneficial feedback for the group. *Data from a team member is sometimes more acceptable to a group than from a trainer.*

There is often useful learning for observers, who may notice behaviours more clearly when separated from the group. They may also see solutions that are missed by the group, which can demonstrate the lesson learned from getting too close to a problem.

If delegates are asked to observe they should be given some guidelines on how to behave while observing and be supported in their feedback. It may be useful to give them some specific questions to answer or a checklist, as recommended in the main text.

Figure 8.2 *Observation by group members*

The facilitator does this by:

- Observing group behaviour.
- Assisting the review process.
- Supplementing review.
- Reducing barriers to effective review.

We will examine each of these topics in some detail:

Observing Group Behaviour

Although this looks easy to outsiders, it is surprisingly difficult to do well and should be practised (see Figure 8.3). Part of the difficulty is because of what behavioral scientists call the Hawthorne Effect – a phenomenon first recognized during an on-the-spot study of working conditions in which the very act of someone taking an interest in them had a positive effect on workers' performance.

At its most gross, the effect can be observed in the behaviour of people in the background of outside broadcasts, who transform from perfectly normal passers-by into impressionists keen to treat the viewing millions to imitations of Charles Laughton as Quasimodo, just as soon as the cameras start to roll.

Group observation is a difficult and surprisingly tiring task. It is also a necessary skill for MDO. We therefore suggest that it is better to practise it before having to use it on a programme. The best way to do this is to watch people working at a task in groups. This may be at a meeting in the office, around a machine on a factory floor, in a library, laboratory or wherever people meet to work together. Spend 10-minute spells observing what's happening, and retire to somewhere private to reflect on what you saw, and coming to whatever conclusions are appropriate. Its amazing how much we learn just by watching and listening to human interaction. Incidentally, on no account should you attempt to conceal yourself or act furtively. This is a guaranteed method of drawing attention to yourself and gaining a reputation as a snooper.

Figure 8.3 *People-watching practice*

The effect of an observer on groups is nothing like so pronounced, but if handled wrongly can lead to untypical behaviour by the group. It is important to avoid this because if group members have been helped or hindered (or even feel that they have) in performance of the task, then they will not feel that it was a real reflection of how they normally work.

In order to avoid this effect, facilitators should:

- *Control physical movement*: It is a simple but often-ignored fact that if one remains very still, one ceases to be noticed. It even works with wild animals! Although it is very difficult to remain still, it *is* possible to avoid sudden movements which divert the group's attention towards the observer and away from each other and their task. Complete stillness is attainable with practice.

- *Control facial expression*: Although they might deny it, most people are accustomed to reading facial expressions and acting upon what they see. This applies more when observing observers of group activity than in many other areas, so facilitators should work at cultivating a neutral expression. People will otherwise seek cues from the observer in how to complete a task, which will then cease to be entirely their own.

  There are some pitfalls in this – we once knew a tutor who was nicknamed 'Buster Keaton' and 'stoneface' by several groups in succession because his adopted 'neutral' expression was actually an intense scowl. When observing groups, we find that our normal 'relaxed' countenances are most effective.

  One of the simplest tricks in group observation is to avoid the eyes of participants unless addressed directly. Again, it is wrong to do this in an obvious manner and would probably lead to accusations of shiftiness. It is best just to apply the rule in a general way.

- *Respect group space*: One of the easiest ways of becoming too noticeable to a group is to stand too close to them. This is very easy to avoid by standing a short distance – perhaps 15ft (5m) – away from the group, which also has the effect of enabling the observer to see the whole group and its dynamics.

  One of the authors at one point unconsciously developed a habit of standing closer when a group was performing poorly or considering inappropriate actions. This behaviour was noticed by a group, whose feedback helped him to change this unhelpful behaviour – more experiential learning!

- *Respect exercise rules*: Often, particularly during exercises with artificial constraints, an observer can become noticeable to the group and also destroy task credibility by failing to observe the same rules. There may be good reasons – safety for example – for doing so, but as a general rule it is best to work within the constraints of each particular exercise.

- *Allow process to proceed*: It is easy for facilitators to think that their role, particularly in the early part of a programme, is to act as peacemaker, pouring oil on the troubled waters of interpersonal conflict. This is rarely so. The role of facilitators is to observe process and assist review. If conflict arises, it should be allowed to happen. If all is peace and light, then so be it. The only reason to intervene is to avoid pointless psychological abuse or actual physical damage.

Tools to Help Observe Groups

There are a variety of aids to group observation.

Discussion maps: A particularly useful tool when watching discussions, is to write all the delegates' names on a piece of paper in a way which reflects their seating arrangement, and draw a line connecting the names each time a person speaks to someone else. For general remarks, draw a line outwards from the speaker. A pattern will emerge, showing who is doing the talking in the group. It may sometimes be appropriate to share your findings with the group.

Another good use of paper and pencil is to record key verbal interventions word for word. This can be useful for quoting in review.

Detailed notes: Some MDO practitioners find that note-taking makes them obtrusive, and certainly clipboards can be quite off-putting to a group. We have found that small notebooks which can be annotated unobtrusively are good, and we often make additional notes immediately after each exercise. This is quite an effective way to arrive at a good overall picture.

We also know several excellent MDO practitioners who make extremely copious notes, so that their writing rapidly ceases to be obtrusive, becoming part of the accepted background. The extremes seem to work equally well, although the middle course sometimes causes problems. People feel threatened enough when they do something stupid. It is worse if a previously passive trainer whips out a notebook and begins furiously scribbling.

Another useful tip is to record incidents a few minutes after they occur to avoid drawing attention to them.

Checklists These are a useful tool to focus observation. We have devised our own (based on Belbin team types, see Belbin (1981)) and also recommend those based on behaviour analysis categories as pioneered by Neil Rackham and Peter Honey (Rackham and Morgan (1977); Honey (1976)).

Assisting the Review Process

Effective review is useful for a number of reasons:

- To clarify and distil learning.
- Where appropriate, to amplify learning.
- To arrive at better ways of doing things.

There are a wide variety of review techniques, but as a general rule, the more the group feels it has arrived at answers, and the less visible the trainer, the more the group will 'own' the conclusions reached.

Groups can be helped in arriving at effective conclusions in a number of ways:

Planned reflection

It always helps to give groups some opportunity to organize their thoughts and feelings about particular processes. At its simplest, this might be by a request for them to ponder awhile on the task.

More usually, groups are given a series of open questions to answer in small sub-groups. The sub-groups then retire to a quiet place to discuss appropriate answers. The trainer's skill in this situation is limited to the

---

1. List three things that make you happy with the way the group is working, and two things which you would like to improve. Provide reasons.
2. When were you most happy with the group and why? When were you least happy and why?
3. Complete an analysis of the factors helping the group and items impeding its progress.
4. In what ways has the group progressed since arriving on the programme?
5. How relevant is this to the working environment?

Figure 8.4 *'Standby' questions used to provoke groups to consider their performance*

not-inconsiderable one of choosing the right question. It is at this point that the time spent observing the group will pay dividends, as it enables the formulating of highly relevant (although still open) questions. Some suitable 'standby' questions are given in Figure 8.4.

After discussion time, sub-groups can come together to share their perceptions. If these are similar, the will to seek answers to their problems will be strengthened. If there is disagreement some lively sharing of insights can ensue, with the facilitator becoming a key figure in ensuring all voices are heard by acting as chairperson.

The benefits of this approach are clear, although if used exclusively there is a danger that groups may avoid difficult issues, and thus fail to develop.

Open review
Some trainers prefer to review exclusively in full groups, chaired by themselves. They can then ask pointed questions and unearth all the group's problems. This approach certainly ensures that the difficult issues are confronted, but there are some difficulties:

- The trainer is the central figure. This may make him or her feel useful and important, but does not help group ownership of learning.
- At times trainers can be insensitive. They sometimes push groups too hard and generate resistance and an 'us and them' feeling.
- Sessions may be dominated by a few group members, leaving the others as spectators, possibly very bored or frustrated.
- Trainers sometimes seek to expose appropriate process by asking leading questions. As a result they may appear smug and patronizing. This does not help their relationship with the group.

Other approaches to review
There are as many approaches to review as there are trainers. In our experience, a judicious mixture of the two approaches outlined above, making full use of open and probing questions and combined with formal and informal one-to-one discussions, works best.

The alternatives are endless, including dramatic presentations (excellent for consolidating learning and driving it into the memory), group feedback to individuals (very powerful if tactfully done and chaired by a skilled trainer) and 'what we need to do differently' sessions in the form of sales presentations by one half of the group to another.

Supplements to Review

There are a variety of implements which enable groups to identify interpersonal issues, problems and opportunities, and which positively augment the *task–review–resolve–relate back* cycle. These include:

- *Psychometric instruments and other questionnaires:* There are a variety of these, examining a very wide range of human behaviours and characteristics. Well known examples include the Myers-Briggs Type Indicator, 16PF, and OPQ. The publishers of most require some form of training – usually a short residential course, perhaps with a written examination.

  This can be costly, but if a particular psychometric is to be used extensively, it is an excellent investment and crucial in using them successfully. Pirated or plagiarized copies or poorly explained results can be damaging, producing false data and devaluing the instrument. This, in turn, can reflect on the credibility of the programme.

  Some questionnaires are not fully-fledged psychometrics but can add excellent dimensions to programmes. Principal among these are the various editions of the team types self-perception questionnaire, based around Belbin's work. The theory itself is also a useful means of broaching the value of diversity of talent within a team.

  We have found that the Myers-Briggs Type Indicator and other instruments which utilize Jung's (1923) theory of psychological types have added a welcome dimension, and because of their non-threatening nature, lend themselves well to outdoor programmes.

- *Inputs:* A wide variety of inputs are successfully used on MDO programmes. Group performance and course objectives dictate what these might be on any particular programme, and there are so many potential inputs that a comprehensive list is beyond the scope of this book. There are some general rules for guidance:

  - In true experiential training, inputs should act in a supporting role, giving academic credibility to what people have already learned.
  - Inputs should be used sparingly, and when most appropriate. Trainers should always ask themselves questions about whose needs they are meeting. This applies even more if they have particularly favoured inputs. We remember one trainer of whom a client said, 'Of course he works to meet

real needs ... its just that every group he's ever worked with seems to need action-centred leadership...'

- If possible, inputs should be supported by written material. Although trainers sometimes feel that handouts are never read, they do provide useful backup, particularly in the hurly-burly of an MDO programme.

Overcoming Barriers to Effective Review

Many things can impede effective review, although these obstructions can be conveniently subdivided into two categories: trainer-generated problems and group-generated problems.

Trainer-generated problems

A variety of factors can lead to trainers causing review to be more difficult than it would otherwise be. These include:

- *Inexperience* Not merely the province of the young. We find, for example, that those with limited experience of the world of industry sometimes experience difficulty in relating to the problems of delegates. As a result, they can fall into the trap of over-reliance on theory, with consequent loss of credibility and possibly authority. In Elton Mayo's (1933) terms, 'knowledge of' gained through academic endeavour is often not enough. 'Knowledge by acquaintance'– obtained by personal experience – is necessary for true understanding, and thus for true credibility. Experiential trainers should be experienced!
- *Inappropriate exercises* Although exercises always generate process of one type or another, poor design will prevent the desired processes emerging. In our early years, under the pressure of an over-full order book, we ran a course that was highly effective in highlighting interpersonal problems with the group in question. This would have been wonderful, but what the customer wanted was something completely different! A good prospect was thus lost to us, and we learned an expensive lesson – design to fit the needs!
- *Impatience* We once had a client who insisted that we should specify in exact detail what groups would have learned by the end of each day. We protested but he insisted. He also insisted that he give a small input to round-off each day. Instead of the harmlessly avuncular homily we had been led to expect, his input turned into a harangue about how the group was learning the lessons of

experience too slowly, and spelling out what those lessons should have been. He became very unpopular very quickly. Groups learn at their own pace, and a wise facilitator pushes the boundaries only gently. This is particularly true when the course is one in which groups are working through the team-formation process (see Figure 3.2 on p 38). For this to be real, they must move at their own pace, with the trainer watching and helping them identify those moments of truth when they begin to move from one stage to another.

- *Issue-avoidance* Sometimes facilitators feel the need to maintain group harmony at all costs. There are sometimes very good reasons for this, but often conflict is important to group development. By pursuing a 'peace at any price' policy, group development can be stunted.

- *Timetable obsession* MDO practitioners are sometimes tempted to sell courses on the strength of the number of exercises they contain. Problems may then arise when reviews begin to address important issues, but trainers feel the need to stick to the timetable. In such cases, wise trainers treat the process issues as the key, reorganizing schedules as necessary.

- *Trainer ego-building* Trainers run a risk of using review to meet their own, rather than the group's, psychological needs. In doing so they can act like a guru or doctor and prescribe solutions. This behaviour ignores the principles of experiential learning and can be counter-productive.

Delegates often ask trainers for solutions or opinions. This can be flattering, but should be answered carefully. Providing solutions can detract from learning by appearing to devalue a group's efforts and enhance the image of the trainer as an expert and create a false mystique around exercises. A trainer's opinion can be useful feedback for the group, but only if delegates' views are sought first.

We once met a trainer who saw review as an opportunity to demonstrate his intelligence to the world. After prattling to retail butchery managers about the essential 'shalom' of customer service work, he capped his performance by leading an intense discussion about the appropriateness of men demonstrating physical affection for one another. After the ensuing mayhem had died down, we pointed out that the butchers weren't changed by the discussion, and the session had not contributed towards improving their management of people. We can only imagine that he saw review as a way of boosting his somewhat fragile ego, and neither of us was surprised when his employer dispensed with his services.

Group-generated Problems

There are a number of ways in which groups create barriers to their own learning. Most of these barriers are unconsciously created, but occasionally psychological games are played. We will consider these, and recommend strategies for dealing with them.

- *Interesting irrelevancies* An example is the group we knew who liked to spend time speculating how certain unpopular managers in their organization would have fared at particular outdoor tasks. While this was perfectly acceptable coffee-break conversation and included some uproariously funny parodies of the managers concerned, it diverted the group's attention away from its own problems and threatened to spill over into review time. It is tempting for the trainer to court popularity by joining in such sessions, but in the long term this does groups (and clients) a disservice. Once identified, it is easily dealt with by reminding the group of their objective in review.

- *Problem-avoidance* We once met a group with real problems, both in the way they did tasks and in their interpersonal relationships. They were aware enough to have sought training, but once on the course were held back by the most senior team member's anxiety to maintain harmony at all costs. He kept saying things like, 'I think we're getting a bit personal now...' when fellow delegates began to broach difficult issues. They, being polite souls, backed off.

    There was every sign that the programme would continue in this vein, so we intervened by pointing out to the group (without singling out the obstructive delegate) that if they wished to gain from the experience, they might have to suffer the pain of analysing their actions. This support from us was enough, and people found their voices to the lasting benefit of the team.

    On another occasion, we could see that the group's frustration with its leader's inability to face interpersonal issues was beginning to bubble over, and sure enough, after several polite failures the storm broke. We stayed with the group to ensure that things remained constructive, but largely allowed them to talk their problems through and reach some useful conclusions.

- *The blame game* To maintain comfort levels, groups sometimes externalize failure, blaming the task ('It was too difficult for the likes of us!'), the employer ('The only problem we've got is the outfit we work for – always setting us up to fail – even on courses they give us impossible tasks!'), the trainer ('You gave us an exercise that was too difficult!'), other groups ('If they had co-operated, the task might not have been impossible!') and even the weather ('Anyone could have done that one in the dry, but in rain it was impossible!').

Trainers often (and understandably!) feel threatened under such circumstances, and react defensively. This is usually an inappropriate response, and we recommend that in such circumstances facilitators should remain – or at least appear – calm, and by open and probing questions, gently nudge the group into examining its own performance.

An exception to this is when something has genuinely gone wrong – perhaps a clue in an orienteering exercise being put in the wrong place. In this case, be honest and deal with the problem. After a cooling-off period, move back into process review.

A client tells us of a course in which the trainers clumsily attempted to conceal a technical error, resulting in them losing forever the trust of the group ... and eventually losing the customer to us. Honesty sometimes really is the best policy!

Effective Review

Process review is important for amplifying and focusing learning on MDO programmes. It can turn a mediocre series of exercises into valuable learning.

It is often a neglected factor, or just something tacked on to the end of an outdoor exercise. Yet review should be:

- process (not task) based;
- an integral part of overall programme design;
- something in which trainers are able to demonstrate real skill and interest;
- trainee (not trainer!) centred;
- at the pace of the group, not forced.

If these conditions exist, review is an indispensable tool of MDO.

ACTIVITY 8

A group is given the task of collecting and assembling the parts of a model aeroplane for cash. They possess the relevant maps, and have received instruction in their use. Although they know that the parts are split between ten sites they only know the location of four, the location of the other six being available at those or subsequent sites. All sites are near public telephones, which are marked on the map. The group room has a telephone. The area is quite mountainous, so mobile telephones are only of very limited use.

The group is also given a time/completion chart (see below) and told that if they wish to use vehicles, two (driven by staff members) are available to them at a cost of 5p per mile. The usual safety rules apply: delegates leaving the training room must do so in groups of two or more, and stay together. The group may cash-in at any time.

Time/completion chart

Time taken (minutes)	Percentage completed									
	10	20	30	40	50	60	70	80	90	100
30	0	0	0	4	5	6	7	8	9	10
45	0	0	0	3	4	5	6	7	8	9
60	0	0	0	2	3	4	5	6	7	8
75	0	0	0	1	2	3	4	5	6	7
90	-1	0	0	0	1	2	3	4	5	6
105	-2	-1	0	0	0	1	2	3	4	5
120	-3	-2	-1	0	0	0	1	2	3	4
135	-4	-3	-2	-1	0	0	0	1	2	3
150	-5	-4	-3	-2	-1	0	0	0	1	2

Income/expenditure in £

Consider the ramifications and complications of this exercise. What problems might the group face? What decisions might they need to make? What is the learning potential?

Appendix 1

Recommended Qualifications for Outdoor Pursuits Trainers

The qualifications listed below are those currently recommended for the discipline in question. While standards of testing and examination are high, fools can pass exams by working hard. Practical tests – which of necessity are of finite duration – are also no guarantee of responsibility, so please treat qualifications as a useful but by no means perfect guide. Use your discretion as well!

Qualifications for Britain are as follows:

Expeditioning/Geographical Exercises

No formal qualifications exist for non-mountainous terrain. We recommend that you use instructors who can demonstrate skill and experience with maps, and, where driving is required, a clean driving licence.

The nationally recognized qualification for work in wild country where walkers are dependent upon themselves and remote from any intermediate help is the **Mountain Leader Certificate**, awarded by the Mountain Walking Leader Training Board (MLTB). This award has two levels: **MLC (summer)** and **MLC (winter)** for the appropriate seasons.

MLC holders are required to hold a recognized first-aid certificate, although it is always worth enquiring whether this is up-to-date.

Climbing and Abseiling

In the past, this has been left to local education authorities, whose outdoor centres have set standards expected from organizations supervising the activities of groups working under the banner of their youth or education sections. This rather haphazard arrangement has now been supplanted by the **Single Pitch Supervisors' Award (SPSA)** granted by the

MLTB. This award, which includes a relevant first-aid qualification, covers holders to supervise single-pitch climbing and abseiling, but is not valid for instructing the leading of climbs, or instructing the setting-up of belays.

Water-based Activities

Canoes and kayaks

Where safety support (for example on rafting or river-crossing exercises) or the activity itself involves canoes or kayaks, the British Canoe Union has for many years set national standards. These are at several levels.

The BCU Instructor's Certificate is relevant to 'flat water' activities, and includes either the Canoe Safety Test or the Royal Life Saving Society Life Saving Award, Grade 2, or its equivalents. Basic First Aid and Expired Air Resuscitation (EAR) are included in the BCU Instructor's Certificate.

For moving water activities, the **BCU Senior Instructor's Certificate** is more appropriate, including as it does the full Rescue Test, or RLSS Bronze Medallion, or their equivalents. This involves basic first aid, EAR and External Cardiac Compression (ECC). Such a person is a qualified lifesaver.

Sailing Vessels

The Royal Yacht Association sets the standard for all sizes of sailing vessels. These include the **RYA Dinghy Sailing Instructor's Certificate** for small craft, and the **RYA Sailing Instructor's Certificate** – not awarded until significant experience as a ship master has been gained.

Caving and Spelaeology

The fully recognized national qualification awarded by the National Caving Association is the **Caving Instructor's Certificate (CIC)**. A holder of this award can instruct groups in any caving area of Britain, up to very high standards of caving difficulty.

Acceptable in any particular region is the **Local Cave Leader Assessment (LCL)**, awarded in much the same way as the local climbing instructor awards. The LCL for each region is divided into two stages. Stage 1 qualifies holders to lead and supervise *but not to instruct* a group in a walk in/walk out cave with no pitches. A Stage 2 holder is qualified to lead and supervise *but not to instruct* a group in a cave system with a pitch of no more than 50 ft(15m) using ladder and lifeline technique. Both stages of LCL are qualified first aiders.

First Aid

The following award certificates: British Red Cross Society, St John Ambulance Brigade, St Andrew's Ambulance Brigade. **The First Aid at Work Certificate** is approved by the Health & Safety Executive.

US Equivalents

US Equivalents to British standards can be found by consulting the American Alliance of Health, Physical Education, Recreation and Dance at 1900 Association Drive, Reston, Virginia VA22091. Their telephone number is 703 476 3400, and they can be reached by faxing 703 476 9527.

Recommended Qualifications for Development Training

At the time of going to press there are no nationally or internationally accepted qualifications for development trainers. This situation is likely to change, as a working party has been established to develop a framework of vocational qualifications, and is looking at both 'hard', ie outdoor, and 'soft', ie review and groupwork skills.

Despite the slightly narrow composition of this working party, dominated by members of the rather insular Development Training Agencies Group (DTAG), and rather too much emphasis on the outdoors, it is to be hoped that a worthwhile and realistic structure of qualifications will soon emerge.

Appendix 2

Activities and Some Possible Answers

ACTIVITY 1 (p23)

His role in the business game could have had a number of outcomes, such as:

- Deciding he was a high flier and frustrated in his current role.
- Coming to the conclusion that such business games are unrealistic and therefore of limited value.

At the time, the experience was like an industrial version of those role playing games in which suburban youths are able to shake off the angst of adolescence for a few hours by becoming Viking warriors or trolls – enjoyable and refreshing but of little help in day-to-day life.

The exception to this general point is a very valid one. At the height of his roaring success, the author's behaviour towards competitors became arrogant to the point of offensiveness. They reacted in a very sensible way by setting up a cartel against him. Only the exercise of unfeasible amounts of charm enabled him to maintain his company's leading position.

The lesson was: What goes around comes around; your personal actions *do* have an effect on business – a lesson he hopes he will never forget.

ACTIVITY No 2 (p34)

Potential gains for delegates could include:

- increased self reliance;
- heightened team spirit;

- the development of a strongly supportive atmosphere;
- recognition of strengths and weaknesses;
- practice in persuasion and negotiation;
- ability to look for alternative solutions.

Possible benefits for their employers might include:

- a tightly knit and loyal team;
- practice in risk assessment and decision making;
- more self-confident managers.

Potential risks include:

- elitism and isolation for some team members;
- inappropriate exposure to peer pressure;
- alienation from the whole programme;
- destructive criticism;
- unnecessary group conflict;
- mistrust of tutors.

ACTIVITY 3 (p51)

Potential gains for delegates could include:

- conquering personal fears;
- heightened team spirit;
- the development of a strongly supportive atmosphere;
- recognition of some strengths and weaknesses;
- practice in persuasion.

Possible benefits for their employers might include:

- a tightly knit and loyal team;
- more self-confident managers.

Potential risks include:

- elitism and isolation for some team members;
- inappropriate exposure to peer pressure;
- alienation from the whole programme;
- destructive criticism;
- unnecessary group conflict;
- over-reliance on tutors and other 'experts'.

ACTIVITY 4 (p66)

Potential gains for delegates could include:

- practice in resource management;
- heightened team spirit;
- the development of a strongly supportive atmosphere;
- recognition of relative and varied strengths;
- practice in persuasion and negotiation;
- ability to look for alternative solutions;
- ability to avoid internal competition, seeking co-operation instead;
- practice in use of action-centred leadership;
- trust of each other;
- respect for other people's personal needs.

Possible benefits for their employers might include:

- a tightly knit and loyal team;
- practice in decision making;
- increased self-confidence and trust in managers.

Potential risks include:

- elitism and isolation for some team members;
- inappropriate exposure to peer pressure.

Possible review issues might include:

- attitude to other working groups;
- balancing task, team and individual needs;
- role assignment and involvement;
- benefits of support;
- the point at which encouragement becomes inappropriate and turns into pressure.

ACTIVITY 5 (p75)

On the face of it, such an outburst would be a perfect way of wrecking the course before it began ... and a way for the manager concerned to lose every shred of personal credibility with his people.

The issue can, however, be made to help the group by allowing it to become a topic for discussion, encouraging (but not too hard!) articulation of the pain it has caused, thus enabling the lesson to be absorbed by the leader that people work better when they are able to be themselves rather than a pale copy of their manager.

127

In some cases (and often as courses progress people become much more open with each other) it is also possible to explore with the manager why he or she has behaved in such a way, and to uncover things which have negatively affected their working relationships for years.

Unpromising behaviour such as that mentioned in this case can often be the key for deeply meaningful review, and should be seen as process to be dealt with, not feared as a hindrance.

Beware of extreme 'process spotting', however. It is easy to lose a group's sympathy by pushing too hard and imposing the facilitator's view on to the group.

ACTIVITY 6 (p88)

Likely review outcomes are:

- appropriateness of leadership style;
- value of planning;
- importance of full group involvement;
- need for progress monitoring.

Learning for leader and group might include:

- the dangers of assumptions;
- to challenge decisions;
- to consider others;
- to assess relevance of experience.

ACTIVITY 7 (p107)

Outcomes from review might include:

- recognition of the importance of planning;
- awareness of collective responsibility;
- an examination of strategies for dealing with failure;
- increased respect for the manager;
- an insight into assertive leadership styles;
- a recognition of the value of encouragement.

Perceptions of the leader:

- Seen as supportive. (This is actually how the group – rightly – saw her. If people have given their all, the last thing they need is criticism. Perhaps in the cold light of day, but not in the heat of the moment!)
- There may have been some risk that the group perceived their manager as weak.

ACTIVITY 8 (p121)

Possible problems include:

- misunderstanding of sub-teams' tasks or authority;
- communicating changes of plan to sub-teams;
- sub-teams not bothering to communicate with the centre, thus wasting time and mileage money;
- the group (especially sub-groups in the field) fail to take account of time constraints, and finish with a completed task but a loss sustained.

Necessary decisions:

- when to cash in;
- how much to use the transport;
- how many sub-teams to form and their membership.

Learning potential:

- clear communication;
- delegation of authority;
- decision making;
- planning.

Appendix 3

An Example of MDO used for Organization Development

The Background

A national trading society reorganized and centralized its support departments, including a unit which provided a social, cultural and educational service to its members.

Before the reorganization, individual officers had each reported to a local general manager who, responsible for a host of other things, usually considered their work to be a side-issue, and left them largely to their own devices.

They now reported – through four area co-ordinators – to their own national manager. On paper, a little freedom of action had been lost but a lot of group cohesiveness had been gained.

The reality was less simple. The newly created team was composed of individualists who strongly resisted authority, displaying little energy in centrally organized initiatives but great commitment to their own tasks. They wanted to work as they had always done.

After considering a number of options, the national manager called us in and we agreed to run two programmes, one for himself and the area co-ordinators, and one for the whole team. The reason for the 'top team' programme was to reinforce their already-existing commitment to each other before moving on to the real area of difficulty.

The top team programme worked extremely well; the participants demonstrated real commitment to each other and the mission of their department. They completed a variety of quite challenging tasks and demonstrated all the team skills anyone could wish for. These included:

- practical support for each other;
- a willingness to listen to each other (two-way);
- positive energy;
- appropriate humour (neither cynical nor task-detractive).

They also addressed the matter of the department's prospective role, envisioning a much more proactive and cohesive future. At the end of the three-day programme we had uncovered a set of attitudes which revealed a group of people who had a clear understanding of, and commitment to, each other and the department's future role.

The second programme was slightly different. The majority certainly wanted to be positive and proactive but were impeded in this by a vociferous minority who derived enjoyment from seeing tasks fail. This group devoted energy and skill to blame-placing, directed particularly towards the national manager.

Such a situation is an uncomfortable one for trainers. We feel pressure to either expose the troublemakers or smooth ruffled feelings. It takes real skill *not* to intervene too often. On this occasion heavy tutor-intervention was not the answer, because the group itself began to deal with its own problems, unmasking and isolating troublemakers in more powerful ways than those available to any outsider. Our role was reduced to:

- asking open questions (no probes needed!)
- making sure that the same ground was not covered too often during discussions.

What had started as a fairly cosy teambuilding exercise turned into a major opportunity for departmental development, and led to a process of trust- and identity-building which in its turn has led to the department becoming one which has contributed strongly to the improving image of its parent organization.

The Lesson for Trainers

MDO can be really effective in aiding the human side of Organizational Development. When people talk about 'teambuilding' or 'increasing personal flexibility', they are often hinting at OD, rather than simple personal development. It is important that trainers working on MDO understand this, or they may be doomed to ineffectuality and disappointment.

References and Further Reading

Adair, J (1983) *Effective Leadership – a Self-development Manual*, Gower, Farnborough.

Belbin, R M (1981) *Management Teams – Why they Succeed or Fail*, Heinemann, Oxford.

Briggs-Myers, I (1980) *Gifts Differing*, Consulting Psychologists Press, Palo Alto.

Briggs-Myers, I (1962) *The Myers-Briggs Type Indicator*, Consulting Psychologists Press, Palo Alto.

Creswick, C and Williams R (1979) Untitled paper on MDO, Food, Drink and Tobacco ITB.

Fayol, H (1916) Administration Industrielle et Generale, SIM, Paris. (Translation: Storrs, C (1949) *General and Industrial Administration*, Pitman, London.)

Fraser, G M (1970) *The General Danced at Dawn*, Barrie & Jenkins, London.

Herzberg, F J (1959) *The Motivation to Work*, Wiley, New York.

Honey, P (1976) *Face to Face*, Institute of Personnel Management, London.

James, D (ed.) (1958) *Outward Bound*, Routledge and Kegan Paul, London.

Johnson, D W and Johnson, F P (1975), *Joining Together*, Prentice-Hall, New Jersey.

Jung, C G (1923) *Psychological Types*, Harcourt, New York.

Kearney, A T (1991) *Total Quality: Time to Take Off the Rose Tinted Spectacles*, London.

Kolb D A (1976) *The Learning Style Inventory*, McBer and Co, Boston.

Lewin, K (1935) *A Dynamic Theory of Personality*, McGraw Hill, New York.

Lewis, R and Parker, C (1981) *Beyond the Peter Principle – managing successful transitions, Journal of European Industrial Training*, **5**, 6.

Lowe, P and Lewis, R (1992) *Individual Excellence*, Kogan Page, London.

Maslow, A (1954) *Motivation and Personality*, Harper & Row, New York.

Mayo, G E (1933) *The Human Problems of Industrial Civilisation*, Macmillan, New York.

Mortlock, C J (1978) *Adventure Education*, Keswick Ferguson, London.

Pollard, H R (1974) *Developments in Management Thought*, Heinemann, Oxford.

Rackham, N and Morgan, T (1977) *Behaviour Analysis in Training*, McGraw Hill, London.

Roethlisberger, F J and Dickson W J (1939) *Management and the Worker*, Harvard University Press, Cambridge, MA.

Stewart, V and Stewart, A (1978) *Managing the Manager's Growth*, Gower, Aldershot.

Taylor, F W (1911) *Principles of Scientific Management*, Harper and Brothers, New York.

Tuckman, B W (1965) 'Development sequence in small groups', *The Psychological Bulletin*.

Woodcock, M (1979) *Team Development Manual*, Gower, Aldershot.

Index